HOW
THEY SUCCEEDED

HOW THEY SUCCEEDED

Life Stories of Successful Men Told by Themselves

by

ORISON SWETT MARDEN

Editor of "Success." Author of "Winning Out," Etc., Etc.

Illustrated

GYAN

Published by

Gyan Publishing House
5, Ansari Road
Daryaganj, New Delhi-110002
Phone: 011-47034999, 9811692060
E-mail: books@gyanbooks.com

Distribution Network
gyanbooks.com
India, USA, Canada, UK, Australia, France

ISBN : 978-81-212-4973-7 (PB)
First Published, 1901

2nd Impression 2021

Printed at: Gyan Press, Delhi.

How they Succeeded
Life Stories of Successful Men Told by Themselves
Author: Orison Swett Marden

HOW THEY SUCCEEDED

LIFE STORIES *of* SUCCESSFUL MEN TOLD *by* THEMSELVES

By ORISON SWETT MARDEN

EDITOR *of* "SUCCESS." AUTHOR *of* "WINNING OUT," ETC., ETC.

ILLUSTRATED

CONTENTS

CHAPTER I

CHAPTER II

Contents

Contents

Contents

Contents

Contents

CHAPTER XII

Contents

CHAPTER XIII

CHAPTER XIV

CHAPTER XV

Contents

CHAPTER XVI

Contents

CHAPTER XVII

CHAPTER XVIII

Contents

Contents

CHAPTER XXII

INTRODUCTORY NOTE

THE GREAT INTEREST manifested in the life-stories of successful men and women, which have been published from time to time in the magazine SUCCESS, has actuated their production in book form. Many of these sketches have been revised and rewritten, and new ones have been added. They all contain the elements that make men and women successful; and they are intended to show that character, energy, and an indomitable ambition will succeed in the world, and that in this land, where all men are born equal and have an equal chance in life, there is no reason for despair. I believe that the ideal book for youth should deal with concrete examples; for that which is taken from real life is far more effective than that which is culled from fancy. Character-building, its uplifting, energizing force, has been made the basic principle of this work.

To all who have aided me I express a grateful acknowledgment; and to none more than to those whose life-stories are here related as a lesson to young people. Among those who have given me special assistance in securing those life-stories are, Mr. Harry Steele Morrison, Mr. J. Herbert Welch, Mr. Charles H. Garrett, Mr. Henry Irving Dodge, and Mr. Jesse W. Weik. I am confident that the remarkable exhibit of successful careers made in this book — careers based on sound business principles and honesty — will meet with appreciation on the part of the reading public.

ORISON SWETT MARDEN.

I

MARSHALL FIELD

THIS world-renowned merchant is not easily accessible to interviews, and he seeks no fame for his business achievements. Yet, there is no story more significant, none more full of encouragement and inspiration for youth.

In relating it, as he told it, I have removed my own interrogations, so far as possible, from the interview.

" I was born in Conway, Massachusetts," he said, " in 1835. My father's farm was among the rocks and hills of that section, and not very fertile. All the people were poor in those days. My father was a man who had good judgment, and he made a success out of the farming business. My mother was of a more intellectual bent. Both my parents were anxious that their boys should amount to something in life, and their interest and care helped me.

"I had but few books, scarçely any to speak of. There was not much time for literature. Such books as we had, I made use of.

"I had a leaning toward business, and took up with it as early as possible. I was naturally of a saving disposition: I had to be. Those were saving times. A dollar looked very big to us boys in those days; and as we had difficult labor in earning it, we did not quickly spend it. I however,

DETERMINED NOT TO REMAIN POOR."

"Did you attend both school and college?"

"I attended the common and high schools at home, but not long. I had no college training. Indeed, I cannot say that I had much of any public school education. I left home when seventeen years of age, and of course had not time to study closely.

"My first venture in trade was made as clerk in a country store at Pittsfield, Massachusetts, where everything was sold, including dry-goods. There I remained for four years, and picked up my first knowledge of business. I

SAVED MY EARNINGS AND ATTENDED STRICTLY TO BUSINESS,

and so made those four years valuable to me.

Before I went West, my employer offered me a quarter interest in his business if I would remain with him. Even after I had been here several years, he wrote and offered me a third interest if I would go back.

"But I was already too well placed. I was always interested in the commercial side of life. To this I bent my energies; and

I ALWAYS THOUGHT I WOULD BE A MERCHANT.

"In Chicago, I entered as a clerk in the dry-goods house of Cooley, Woodsworth & Co., in South Water street. There was no guarantee at that time that this place would ever become the western metropolis; the town had plenty of ambition and pluck, but the possibilities of greatness were hardly visible."

It is interesting to note in this connection how closely the story of Mr. Field's progress is connected with Chicago's marvelous growth. The city itself in its relations to the West, was

AN OPPORTUNITY.

A parallel, almost exact, may be drawn between the individual career and the growth of the town. Chicago was organized in 1837, two years after Mr. Field was born on the far-off farm in New England, and the place then had a population of a little more than four thousand. In 1856, when Mr. Field, fully equipped for a successful mercantile career, became a resident of the future metropolis of the West, the population had grown to little more than eighty-four thousand. Mr. Field's prosperity advanced with the growth of the city; with Chicago he was stricken but not crushed by the great fire of 1871; and with Chicago he advanced again to higher achievement and far greater prosperity than before the calamity.

"What were your equipments for success when you started as a clerk here in Chicago, in 1856?"

"Health and ambition, and what I believe to be sound principles;" answered Mr. Field. "And here I found that in a growing town, no one had to wait for promotion. Good business qualities were promptly discovered, and men were pushed forward rapidly.

"After four years, in 1860, I was made a partner, and in 1865, there was a partial reorganization, and the firm consisted after that of Mr. Leiter, Mr. Palmer and myself (Field, Palmer, and Leiter). Two years later Mr. Palmer withdrew, and until 1881, the style of the firm was Field, Leiter & Co. Mr. Leiter retired in that year, and since then it has been as at present (Marshall Field & Co.)."

"What contributed most to the great growth of your business?" I asked.

"To answer that question," said Mr. Field, "would be to review the condition of the West from the time Chicago began until the fire in 1871. Everything was coming this way; immigration, railways and water traffic, and Chicago was enjoying 'flush' times.

"There were things to learn about the country, and the man who learned the quickest fared the best. For instance, the comparative newness of rural communities and settlements made a knowledge of local solvency impossible. The old State banking system prevailed, and speculation of every kind was rampant.

A CASH BASIS

"The panic of 1857 swept almost everything away except the house I worked for, and *I learned that the reason they survived was because they understood the nature of the new country, and did a cash business.* That is, they bought for cash, and sold on thirty and sixty days; instead of giving the customers, whose financial condition you could hardly tell anything about, all the time they wanted. *When the panic came, they had no debts, and little owing to them,* and so they weathered it all right. *I learned what I consider my best lesson, and that was to do a cash business.*"

"What were some of the *principles* you applied to your business?" I questioned.

"*I made it a point that all goods should be exactly what they were represented to be. It was a rule of the house that an exact scrutiny of the quality of all goods purchased should be maintained, and that nothing was to induce the house to place upon the market any line of goods at a shade of variation from their real value. Every article sold must be regarded as warranted, and*

EVERY PURCHASER MUST BE ENABLED TO FEEL SECURE."

"Did you suffer any losses or reverses during your career?"

"No loss except by the fire of 1871. It swept away everything,—about three and a half millions. We were, of course, protected by insurance, which would have been sufficient against any ordinary calamity of the kind. But the disaster was so sweeping that some of the companies which had insured our property were blotted out, and a long time passed before our claims against others were settled. We managed, however, to start again. There were no buildings of brick or stone left standing, but there were some great shells of horse-car barns at State and Twentieth streets which were not burned, and I hired those. We put up signs announcing that we would continue business uninterruptedly, and then rushed the work of fitting things up and getting in the stock."

"Did the panic of 1873 affect your business?"

"Not at all. We did not have any debts."

"May I ask, Mr. Fields, what you consider to have been

THE TURNING POINT

in your career, — the point after which there was no more danger?"

"Saving the first five thousand dollars I ever had, when I might just as well have spent the moderate salary I made. Possession of that sum, once I had it, gave me *the ability to meet opportunities*. That I consider the turning-point."

"What trait of character do you look upon

as having been the most essential in your career?"

"*Perseverance*," said Mr. Field. But Mr. Selfridge, his most trusted lieutenant, in whose private office we were, insisted upon the addition of "*good judgment*" to this.

"If I am compelled to lay claim to such traits," added Mr. Fields, "it is because I have tried to practise them, and the trying has availed me much. I have tried to make all my acts and commercial moves the result of definite consideration and sound judgment. *There were never any great ventures or risks.* I practised honest, slow-growing business methods, and tried to back them with energy and good system."

At this point, in answer to further questions, Mr. Field disclaimed having overworked in his business, although after the fire of '71 he worked about eighteen hours a day for several weeks:—

"My fortune, however, has not been made in that manner. I believe in reasonable hours, but close attention during those hours. I never worked very many hours a day. People do not work as many hours now as they once did.

The day's labor has shortened in the last twenty years for everyone."

QUALITIES THAT MAKE FOR SUCCESS

"What, Mr. Field," I said, "do you consider to be the first requisite for success in life, so far as the young beginner is concerned?"

"The qualities of *honesty, energy, frugality, integrity,* are more necessary than ever to-day, and there is no success without them. They are so often urged that they have become commonplace, but they are really more prized than ever. And any good fortune that comes by such methods is deserved and admirable."

A COLLEGE EDUCATION AND BUSINESS

"Do you believe a college education for the young man to be a necessity in the future?"

"Not for business purposes. Better training will become more and more a necessity. The truth is, with most young men, a college education means that just at the time when they should be having business principles instilled into them, and be getting themselves energetically pulled together for their life's work, they are sent to college. Then intervenes what many a young man looks back on as the jolliest time of his life,—four years of college. Often when he comes out of college the young man is unfitted by this good time to buckle down to hard work, and the result is a failure to grasp opportunities that would have opened the way for a successful career."

As to retiring from business, Mr. Field remarked:—

" I do not believe that, when a man no longer attends to his private business in person every day, he has given up interest in affairs. He may be, in fact should be, doing wider and greater work. There certainly is no pleasure in idleness. A man, upon giving up business, does not cease laboring, but really does or should do more in a larger sense. He should interest himself in public affairs. There is no happiness in mere dollars. After they are acquired, one can use but a moderate amount. It is given a man to eat so much, to wear so much, and to have so much shelter, and more he cannot use. When money has supplied these, its mission, so far as the individual is concerned, is fulfilled, and man must look further and higher. It is only in the wider public affairs, where money is a moving force toward the general welfare, that the possessor of it can possibly find pleasure, and that only in constantly doing more."

"What," I said, "in your estimation, is the greatest good a man can do?"

'The greatest good he can do is to cultivate himself, develop his powers, in order that he may be of greater use to humanity."

II

BELL TELEPHONE TALK

HINTS ON SUCCESS BY ALEXANDER G. BELL.

EXTREMELY polite, always anxious to render courtesy, no one carries great success more gracefully than Alexander G. Bell, the inventor of the telephone. His graciousness has won many a friend, the admiration of many more, and has smoothed many a rugged spot in life.

A NIGHT WORKER

When I first went to see him, it was about eleven o'clock in the morning, and he was in bed! The second time, I thought I would go somewhat later,—at one o'clock in the afternoon. He was eating his breakfast, I was told; and I had to wait some time. He came in apologizing profusely for keeping me waiting. When I told him I had come to interview him, in behalf of young people, about success—its underlying principles,—he threw back his large head and laughingly said:

"'Nothing succeeds like success.' Success did you say? Why, that is a big subject,—too big a one. You must give me time to think about it; and you having planted the seed in my brain, will have to wait for me."

When I asked what time I should call, he said: "Come any time, if it is only late. I begin my work at about nine or ten o'clock in the evening, and continue until four or five in the morning. Night is a more quiet time to work. It aids thought."

So, when I went to see him again, I made it a point to be late. He cordially invited me into his studio, where, as we both sat on a large and comfortable sofa, he talked long on

THE SUBJECT OF SUCCESS.

The value of this article would be greatly enhanced, if I could add his charming manner of emphasizing what he says, with hands, head, and eyes; and if I could add his beautiful distinctness of speech, due, a great deal, to his having given instruction to deaf mutes, who must read the lips.

"What do you think are the factors of success?" I asked. The reply was prompt and to the point.

PERSEVERANCE APPLIED TO A PRACTICAL END

"Perseverance is the chief; but perseverance must have some practical end, or it does not avail the man possessing it. A person without a practical end in view becomes a crank or an idiot. Such persons fill our insane asylums. The same perseverance that they show in some idiotic idea, if exercised in the accomplishment of something practicable, would no doubt bring success. Perseverance is first, but practicability is chief. The success of the Americans as a nation is due to their great practicability."

"But often what the world calls nonsensical, becomes practical, does it not? You were called crazy, too, once, were you not?"

"There are some things, though, that are always impracticable. Now, take, for instance, this idea of perpetual motion. Scientists have proved that it is impossible. Yet our patent office is continually beset by people applying for inventions on some perpetual motion machine. So the department has adopted a rule whereby a working model is always required of such applicants. They cannot furnish one. The impossible is incapable of success."

"I have heard of people dreaming inventions."

"That is not at all impossible. I am a believer in unconscious cerebration. The brain is working all the time, though we do not know it. At night, it follows up what we think in the daytime. When I have worked a long time on one thing, I make it a point to bring all the facts regarding it together before I retire; and I have often been surprised at the results. Have you not noticed that, often, what was dark and perplexing to you the night before, is found to be perfectly solved the next morning? We are thinking all the time; it is impossible not to think."

"Can everyone become an inventor?"

"Oh, no; not all minds are constituted alike. Some minds are only adapted to certain things. But as one's mind grows, and one's knowledge of the world's industries widens, it adapts itself to such things as naturally fall to it."

Upon my asking the relation of health to success, the professor replied:—

"I believe it to be a primary principle of success; 'mens sana in corpore sano,'—a sound mind in a sound body. The mind in a weak body produces weak ideas; a strong body gives strength to the thought of the mind. Ill health is due to man's artificiality of living. He lives indoors. He becomes, as it were, a hothouse plant. Such a plant is never as successful as a hardy garden plant is. An outdoor life is necessary to health and success, especially in a youth."

"But is not hard study often necessary to success?"

"No; decidedly not. You cannot force ideas. Successful ideas are the result of slow growth. Ideas do not reach perfection in a day, no matter how much study is put upon them. It is *perseverance* in the pursuit of studies that is really wanted.

CONCENTRATION OF PURPOSE

"Next must come concentration of purpose and study. That is another thing I mean to emphasize. Concentrate all your thought upon the work in hand. The sun's rays do not burn until brought to a focus.

"I am now thinking about flying machines. Everything in regard to them, I pick out and read. When I see a bird flying in the air, I note its manner of flight, as I would not if I were not constantly thinking about artificial flight, and concentrating all my thought and observation upon it. It is like a man who has made the acquaintance of some new word that has been brought forcibly to his notice, although he may have come across it many times before, and not have noticed it particularly.

"*Man is the result of slow growth;* that is why he occupies the position he does in animal life. What does a pup amount to that has gained its growth in a few days or weeks, beside a man who only attains it in as many years. A horse is often a grandfather before a boy has attained his full maturity. The most successful men in the end are those whose success is the result of steady accretion. That intellectuality is more vigorous that has attained its strength gradually. It is the man who carefully advances step by step, with his mind becoming wider and wider,—and progressively better able to grasp any theme or situation,—persevering in what he knows to be practical, and concentrating his thought upon it, who is bound to succeed in the greatest degree.

YOUNG AMERICAN GEESE

"If a man is not bound down, he is sure to succeed. He may be bound down by environment, or by doting parental petting. In Paris, they fatten geese to create a diseased condition of the liver. A man stands with a box of very finely prepared and very rich food beside a revolving stand, and, as it revolves, one goose after another passes before him. Taking the first goose by the neck, he clamps down its throat a large lump of the food, whether the goose will or no, until its crop is well stuffed out, and then he proceeds with the rest in the same very mechanical manner. Now, I think, if those geese had to work hard for their own food, they would digest it better, and be far healthier geese. How many young American geese are stuffed in about the same manner at college and at home, by their rich and fond parents!"

UNHELPFUL READING

"Did everything you ever studied help you to attain success?"

"On the contrary, I did not begin real study until I was over sixteen. Until that time, my principal study was—reading novels." He laughed heartily at my evident astonishment. "They did not help me in the least, for they did not give me an insight into real life. It is only those things that give one a grasp of practical affairs that are helpful. To read novels continuously is like reading fairy stories or "Arabian Nights" tales. It is a butterfly existence, so long as it lasts; but, some day, one is called to stern reality, unprepared."

INVENTIONS IN AMERICA

"You have had experience in life in Europe and in America. Do you think the chances for success are the same in Europe as in America?"

"It is harder to attain success in Europe. There is hardly the same appreciation of progress there is here. Appreciation is an element of success. Encouragement is needed. My thoughts run mostly toward inventions. In England, people are conservative. They are well contented with the old, and do not readily adopt new ideas. Americans more quickly appreciate new inventions. Take an invention to an Englishman or a Scot, and he will ask you all about it, and then say your invention may be all right, but let somebody else try it first.

Take the same invention to an American, and if it is intelligently explained, he is generally quick to see the feasibility of it. America is an inspiration to inventors. It is quicker to adopt advanced ideas than England or Europe. The most valuable inventions of this century have been made in America."

THE ORIENT

"Do you think there is a chance for Americans in the Orient?"

"There is only a chance for capital in trade. American labor cannot compete with Japanese and Chinese. A Japanese coolie, for the hardest kind of work, receives the equivalent of six cents a day; and the whole family, father, mother and children, work and contribute to the common good. A foreigner is only made use of until they have absorbed all his useful ideas; then he is avoided. The Japanese are ahead of us in many things."

ENVIRONMENT AND HEREDITY

"Do you think environment and heredity count in success?"

"Environment, certainly; heredity, not so distinctly. In heredity, a man may stamp out the faults he has inherited. There is no chance for the proper working of heredity. If selection could be carried out, a man might owe much to heredity. But as it is, only opposites marry. Blonde and light-complexioned people marry brunettes, and the tall marry the short. In our scientific societies, men only are admitted. If women who were interested especially in any science were allowed to affiliate with the men in these societies, we might hope to see some wonderful workings of the laws of heredity. A man, as a general rule, owes very little to what he is born with. A man is what he makes of himself.

" Environment counts for a great deal. A man's particular idea may have no chance for growth or encouragement in his community. Real success is denied that man, until he finds a proper environment.

America is a good environment for young men. It breathes the very spirit of success. I noticed at once, when I first came to this country, how the people were all striving for success, and helping others to attain success. It is an inspiration you cannot help feeling. AMERICA IS THE LAND OF SUCCESS."

PROFESSOR BELL'S LIFE STORY

Alexander Graham Bell was born in Edinburgh, Scotland, March 3, 1847. His father, Alexander Melville Bell, now in Washington, D. C., was a distinguished Scottish educator, and the inventor of a system of "visible speech," which he has successfully taught to deaf-mutes. His grandfather, Alexander Bell, became well known by the invention of a method of removing impediments of speech.

The younger Bell received his education at the Edinburgh High School and University; and, in 1867, he entered the University of London. Then, in his twenty-third year, his health failing from over-study, he came with his father to Canada, as he expressed it, "to die." Later, he settled in the United States, becoming first a teacher of deaf-mutes, and subsequently professor of vocal physiology in Boston University. In 1867, he first began to study the problem of conveying articulate sound by electric currents; which he pursued during his leisure time. After nine long years of research and experiment, he completed the first telephone, early in 1876, when it was exhibited at the Centennial Exposition, and pronounced the "wonder of wonders in electric telegraphy." This was the judgment of scientific men who were in a position to judge, and not of the world at large. People regarded it only as a novelty, as a curious scientific toy; and most business men doubted that it would ever prove a useful factor in the daily life of the world, and the untold blessing to mankind it has since become. All this skepticism he had to overcome. "A new art was to be taught to the world, a new industry created, business and social methods revolutionized."

"I WILL MAKE THE WORLD HEAR IT"

"It does speak," cried Sir William Thompson, with fervid enthusiasm; and Bell's father-in-law added: "I will make the world hear it." In less than a quarter of a century, it is conveying thought in every civilized tongue; Japan being the first country outside of the United States to adopt it. In the first eight years of its existence, the Bell Telephone Company declared dividends to the extent of $4,000,000; and the great sums of money the company earns for its stockholders is a subject of current comment and wonder. Some fierce contests have been waged over the priority of his invention, but Mr. Bell has been triumphant in every case.

He has become very wealthy from his invention. He has a beautiful winter residence in Washington; fitted up with a laboratory, and all sorts of electrical conveniences mostly of his own invention. His summer residence is at Cambridge, Massachusetts.

His wife, Mabel, the daughter of the late Gardiner G. Hubbard, is a deaf-mute, of whose education he had charge when she was a child.

Mr. Bell, with one of his beautiful daughters, recently made a visit to Japan. The Order of the Rising Star, the highest order in the gift of the Japanese Emperor, was bestowed upon him. He is greatly impressed by the character of the people; believing them capable of much greater advancement.

Mr. Bell is the inventor of the photophone, aiming to transmit speech by a vibratory beam of light. He has given much time and study to problems of multiplex telegraphy, and to efforts to record speech by photographing the vibrations of a jet of water.

Few inventors have derived as much satisfaction and happiness from their achievements as Mr. Bell. In this respect, his success has been ideal, and in impressive contrast with the experience of Charles Goodyear, the man who made india-rubber useful, and of some other well-known inventors, whose services to mankind brought no substantial reward to themselves.

Mr. Bell is in nowise spoiled by his good fortune; but is the same unpretending person today, that he was before the telephone made him wealthy and famous.

III

Why the American People Like Helen Gould

MISS HELEN GOULD has won a place for herself in the hearts of Americans such as few people of great wealth ever gain. Her strong character, commonsense, and high ideals, have made her respected by all, while her munificence and kindness have won for her the love of many.

Upon my arrival at her Tarrytown home, I was made to feel that I was welcome, and everyone who enters her presence feels the same. The grand mansion, standing high on the hills overlooking the Hudson, has a home-like appearance. Chickens play around the little stone cottage at the grand entrance, and the grounds are not unlike those of any other country house, with trees in abundance, and beautiful lawns. There are large beds of flowers, and in the gardens all the summer vegetables were growing.

Miss Helen Gould

Miss Gould takes a very great interest in her famous greenhouses, the gardens, the flowers, and the chickens, for she is a home-loving woman. It is a common thing to see her in the grounds, digging and raking and planting, like some farmer's girl. That is one reason why her neighbors all like her; she seems so unconscious of her wealth and station.

A FACE FULL OF CHARACTER

When I entered Lyndhurst, she came forward to meet me in the pleasantest way imaginable. Her face is not exactly beautiful, but has a great deal of character written upon it, and it is very attractive. She held out her hand for me to shake in the good old-fashioned way, and then we sat down in the wide hall to talk. Miss Gould was dressed very simply. Her gown was of dark cloth, close-fitting, and her skirt hung several inches above the ground, for she is a believer in short skirts for walking. Her entire costume was very becoming. She never over-dresses, and her garments are neat, and naturally of excellent quality.

HER AMBITIONS AND AIMS

In the conversation that followed, I was permitted to learn much of her ambitions and aims. She is ambitious to leave an impression on the world by good deeds well done, and this ambition is gratified to the utmost. She is modest about her work.

"I cannot find that I am doing much at all," she said, "when there is so very much to be done. I suppose I shouldn't expect to be able to do everything, but I sometimes feel that I want to, nevertheless."

A MOST CHARMING CHARITY

One of her most charming charities is "Woody Crest," two miles from Lyndhurst, a haven of delight where some twoscore waifs are received at a time for a two weeks' visit.

Years before Miss Gould's name became associated throughout the country with charity, she was doing her part in trying to make a world happier. Every summer she was hostess to scores of poor children, who were guests at one of the two Gould summer homes; little people with pinched, wan faces, and crippled children from the tenements, were taken to that home and entertained. They came in relays, a new company arriving once in two weeks, the number of children thus given a taste of heaven on earth being limited only by the capacity of the Gould residence. This was her first, and, I am told, her favorite charity.

Little children do things naturally. It was when a child that Helen Gould commenced the work that has given her name a sacred significance. When a little girl, she could see the less fortunate little girls passing the great Gould home on Fifth avenue, and she pitied them and loved them, and from her own allowance administered to their comfort.

" My father always encouraged me in charitable work," she writes a friend. How much the American people owe to that encouragement. A frown from that father, idolized as he was by his daughter, would have frosted and killed that budding philanthropy which has made a great fortune a fountain of joy, and carried sunshine into many lives.

" Woody Crest " is a sylvan paradise, a nobly wooded hill towering above the sumptuous green of Westchester, a place with wild flowers and winding drives, and at its crest a solid mansion built of the native rock. One can look out from its luxuriant lawns to the majestic Hudson, or turn aside into the shadiest of nooks among the trees. What a place for the restful breezes to fan the tired brows from the tenements. Do the little folks enjoy it? Ask them, and their eyes will sparkle with gladness for answer. Ask those, too, who are awaiting their turn in hot New York, and watch the eagerness of their anticipation. For two long and happy weeks they become as joyous as mortals are ever permitted to be.

Miss Gould has a personal oversight of the place, and, by her frequent visits, makes friends with the wee visitors, who look upon her as a combination of angel and fairy godmother. Every day, a wagonette drawn by two horses takes the children, in relays, for long drives into the country. Amusements are provided, and some of those who remain for an entire season at Woody Crest are instructed in different branches. Twice a month some of the older boys set the type for a little magazine which is devoted to Woody Crest matters. There are several portable cottages erected there, one for the sick, one for servants' sleeping rooms, and a third for a laundry.

And the munificent hostess of these children of the needy gets her reward in eyes made bright, in cheeks made ruddy, in the "God bless you," that falls from the lips of grateful parents.

All winter long, instead of closing "Woody Crest" and waiting for the summer sunshine to bring about a return of her charitable opportunities, Miss Gould has kept the place running at full expense. During the winter she herself occupies her town residence. Ordinarily she would not keep "Woody Crest" open longer than Thanksgiving Day, but in the past winter fifteen small boys were entertained for six months. Six of these were cripples, and nine were sound of limb. Though it required many servants, I am told that the little guests were given as much consideration as the same number of grown people would have received. They had nurses and physicians for those who needed them, governesses and instructors for those who were well.

HER PRACTICAL SYMPATHY FOR THE LESS FAVORED

When, one day, I was privileged to meet Miss Gould at Woody Crest, I saw a hundred children scattered around the lawn in front of the stately mansion. It had been an afternoon of labor and anxiety on her part, for she felt the responsibility of entertaining and caring for so many little ones. As she finally cooled herself on the piazza and looked at her little charges romping around on the lawn, I asked her if she thought any of the little ones before her would ever make their mark in the world.

"That's hard to say," she replied, after a moment's hesitation, "but no one can tell what may be in children until they have grown up and developed. But the hardest thing to me is to see genius struggling under obstacles and in surroundings that would discourage almost anybody. I do not see, for my part, how any child from the poorest tenements could ever grow up and develop into strong, successful men or women. Many of them, of course, have no gifts or endowments to do this, but even if they had, the surroundings are enough to stifle every spark of ambition in them. It is a mystery to me how they can preserve such bright and eager faces. What would we do if we were brought up in such environments! I know I should never be able to survive it, and would never succeed in rising above my surroundings. And it is harder on the girls than the boys! The boys can go forth into the world and probably secure a position which in time will bring them different companionship and surroundings; but the poor girls have so few opportunities. They must drudge and drag along for the bare necessities of life. My heart aches sometimes for them, and I wish I had the power to lighten the burdens of everyone."

"The hardest thing, I suppose, is to see real ability fighting against odds, with no one to help and encourage?"

"Yes, that seems the worst, and I think we all ought to make it possible for such ones to get a little encouragement and help. When a boy is deserving of credit it should be given unstintedly. It goes a long way toward making him more hopeful for the future. We don't as a rule receive enough encouragement in this world. Certainly not the poor. Everybody seems so busy and intent upon making his own way in the world that he forgets to drop a word of cheer for those who have not been so fortunate by birth or surroundings."[1]

For a number of years, Miss Gould has supported certain beds in the Babies' Shelter, in connection with the Church of the Holy Communion, New York, and the Wayside Day Nursery, near Bellevue Hospital, has always

[1] NOTE.—For four paragraphs preceding I am indebted to GEORGE ETHELBERT WALSH, whose interview was published in the *Boston Transcript,* Oct. 12, 1900.

found in her a good friend. Once a year she makes a tour through the day nurseries of New York, noting the special needs of each, and often sending money or materials for meeting those needs.

PERSONAL ATTENTION TO AN UNSELFISH SERVICE

Her charities, says Mr. Walsh, in the article above cited, are probably the most practical on record. She does not go "slumming," as so many fashionable girls do, but she does go and investigate personal charities herself and apply the medicine as she thinks best. She puts herself out in more ways to relieve distress around than she would to accommodate her wealthiest friend. Not only has she always pitied the sufferers in the world less fortunate than herself, but she has always had a great desire to help those struggling for a living in practical ways to get along. It is this side of her noble work that stands out most conspicuously to-day. The public realizes for the first time that this young woman, who first came into actual fame at the time of our war with Spain, has been supporting and encouraging young people in different parts of the country for years past. These protéges are all worthy of her patronage, and *they have been sought out by her. Not one has ever approached Miss Gould for help, and in fact such an introduction would undoubtedly operate against her inclination to help them. She has discovered them;* and then through considerable tact and discretion obtained from them their ambitious desires and hopes. Through equally good tact and sense she has then placed them in positions where they could work out their own destinies without feeling that they were accepting charity. This is distinctly what Miss Gould wishes to avoid in helping her little protéges. She does not offer them charity or do anything to make them dependent upon her if it can be helped. By her money and influence she obtains for them positions which will give them every chance in the world to rise and develop talents which she thinks she has discovered in them.

Some of her protéges, continues Mr. Walsh, have been sent away to schools and colleges. One of the easiest ways to accomplish this is to offer a scholarship in some institution and then place her young protége in such a position that he or she can win it, and in this way have four years of tuition free. Fully a dozen different scholars are now enjoying the benefits of Miss Gould's kindness in this and other respects. Four others have been enabled to attend art schools, and two are studying music under the best teachers through the instrumentality of this young woman. Two of these scholars were literally rescued from the tenement dregs of New York, and they showed such aptitude for study and work that Miss Gould undertook to give them a fair start in the world. Unusual aptitude, brightness, or kindness on the part of children always attract Miss Gould, and she has become the patron saint of more than a hundred. When her name is mentioned they show their interest and concern, not by looks of awe and fear but of eagerness and happiness. Those of their number who have been lifted from their low estate and put in high positions to carve out a life of success through their common patron saint, bring back stories of her kindness and consideration that make the children look upon her as they would the Madonna. But she is a youthful Madonna, and the very idea of posing as such, even before the poor and ignorant of her little friends, would amuse her. Nevertheless, that is the nearest that one can interpret their ideas concerning her.

Miss Gould's beneficiaries have been sometimes aided in obtaining the most advanced schooling in the land; and she visits with equal interest the industrial classes of Berea and the favored students of the College Beautiful.

HER VIEWS UPON EDUCATION

Miss Gould is well educated, and a graduate of a law school. I tried to ascertain her views regarding the education of young women of to-day, and what careers they should follow. This is one of her particular hobbies, and many are the young girls she has helped to attain to a better and more satisfactory life.

"I believe most earnestly in education for women," she said; "not necessarily the higher education about which we hear so much, but a good, common-school education. As the years pass, girls are obliged to make their own way in the world more and more; and to do so, they must have good schooling."

"And what particular career do you think most desirable for young women?"

"Oh, as to careers, there are many that young women follow, nowadays. I think, if I had my own way to make, I should fit myself to be a private secretary. That is a position which attracts nearly every young woman; but, to fill it, she must study hard and learn, and then work hard to keep the place. Then there are openings for young women in the fields of legitimate business. Women know as much about money affairs as men, only most of them have not had much experience. In that field, there are hundreds of things that a woman can do.

THE EVIL OF IDLENESS

"But I don't think it matters much what a girl does so long as she is active, and doesn't allow herself to stagnate. There's nothing, to my mind, so pathetic as a girl who thinks she can't do anything, and is of no use to the world."

HER PATRIOTISM

The late Admiral Philip, he of the "Texas" in the Santiago fight, regarded Miss Gould as an angel, and the sailors of the Brooklyn navy yard fairly worship her. A hustling Y. M. C. A. chap, Frank Smith by name, started a little club-house for "Jack Ashore," near the Brooklyn navy yard. Miss Gould heard of this club, and visited it. At a glance she grasped the meaning, and, on her return home she wrote a letter and a check for fifty thousand dollars, and there sprang from that letter and check, a handsome building in which there are sixty beds, a library, a pipe organ, a smoking-room, and a restaurant. Do you wonder that the "Jackies" adore her, and that the gale that sweeps over the ship out in the open sea is often freighted with the melody of her name?

"When I visited Cuba and Porto Rico," says Congressman Charles B. Landis, of Indiana, — to whom I am greatly indebted in preparing this article,—"I talked with officers and privates everywhere along the journey, visited camps and hospitals in cities and isolated towns, and everywhere it seemed that the sickness and suffering and heart yearning of the American soldier had been anticipated by Helen Gould. Voices that quivered and eyes that moistened at the mention of the name of this young American girl were one continuous tribute to her heart and work. She cannot fully realize how far-reaching have been her efforts."

A business man looks for results. What impressed me most with Miss Gould's work was the visible, tangible results. Every dollar spent by her seemed to go, straight as a cannon-ball, to some mark. Miss Gould has a business head, and is not hysterical in her work. She gives, but follows the gift and sees that it goes to the spot. She has studied results and knows which charity pays a premium in smiles, and tears, and joy, and better life, and very little of her money will be wasted in impracticable schemes. She has a happy faculty of getting in actual touch with conditions, realizing that she cannot hit an object near at hand by aiming at a star.

Miss Gould's practical business sense was beautifully exemplified at Montauk Point. Hundreds of soldiers from the hospitals in Cuba and Porto Rico were suddenly unloaded there. Elsewhere were government supplies — tents and cots and rations,—but there the sick soldiers were without shelter, were hungry, had no medicine, and were sleeping on the ground.

Why? Because of red tape. This young lady appeared in person and amazed the strutters in shoulder-straps and the slaves to discipline by having the sick soldier boys made comfortable on army cots, placed in army tents, and fed on army rations,—and this, too, without any "requisition." She grasped a situation, cut the ropes of theory and introduced practice. From her own purse she provided nurses and dainties, and bundled up scores of soldier boys and sent them to her beautiful villa on the Hudson.

The camp rang with this refrain:—

You're the angel of the camp,
  Helen Gould,
In the sun-rays, in the damp,
On the weary, weary tramp,
To our darkness you're a lamp,
  Helen Gould.

Thoughts of home and gentle things,
  Helen Gould,
To the camp your coming brings;
All the place with music rings
At the rustle of your wings,
  Helen Gould.

"OUR HELEN"

On the day of the Dewey parade in New York, Miss Gould was in front of her house, on a platform she had erected for the small children of certain Asylums. Mayor Van Wyck told Admiral Dewey who she was, and the Admiral stood up in his carriage and bowed to her three times. Then the word went down the line that Miss Gould was there, and every company saluted her as it passed.

But it was when a body of young recruits stopped for a moment before her door that the real excitement began.

"She shan't marry a foreign prince," they cried, tossing their hats and stamping their feet. "She's Helen, our Helen, and she shall not marry a foreign prince."

"AMERICA"

Miss Gould's patriotism is very real and intense, and is not confined to times of war. Two years ago, she caused fifty thousand copies of the national hymn, "America," to be printed and distributed among the pupils of the public schools of New York.

"I believe every one should know that hymn and sing it," she declared, "if he sings no other. I would like to have the children sing it into their very souls, till it becomes a part of them."

She strongly favors patriotic services in the churches on the Sunday preceding the Fourth of July, when she would like to hear such airs as "America," "Hail Columbia," and "The Star Spangled Banner," and see the sacred edifices draped in red, white, and blue.

UNHERALDED BENEFACTIONS

Miss Gould has a strong prejudice against letting her many gifts and charities be known, and even her dearest friends never know " what Helen's doing now." Of course, her great public charities, as when she gives a hundred thousand dollars at a time, are heralded. Her recent gift of that sum to the government, for national defense, has made her name beloved throughout the land; but, had she been able, she would have kept that secret also.

The place Helen Gould now holds in the love and esteem of the republic exemplifies how quickly the nation's heart responds to the touch of gentleness, and how easy it is for wealth to conquer and rise triumphant, if only it be seasoned with common sense and sympathy.

I will not attempt to specify the numerous projects of charity that have been given life and vigor by Miss Gould. I know her gifts in recent years have passed the million-dollar mark.

" It seems so easy to do things for others," said Miss Gould, recently. It is easy to do good, if the doing is natural and without thought of self-glorification.

Miss Gould's views upon "How to Make the Most of Wealth," are well set forth in her admirable letter to Dr. Louis Klopsch, as published in the *Christian Herald*:—

"The Christian idea that wealth is a stewardship, or trust, and not to be used for one's personal pleasure alone, but for the welfare of others, certainly seems the noblest; and those who have more money or broader culture owe a debt to those who have had fewer opportunities.

" And there are so many ways one can help. Children, the sick and the aged especially, have claims on our attention, and the forms of work for them are numerous; from kindergartens, day-nurseries and industrial schools, to 'homes' and hospitals. Our institutions for higher education require gifts in order to do their best work, for the tuition fees do not cover the expense of the advantages offered; and certainly such societies as those in our churches, and the Young Woman's Christian Association and the Young Men's Christian Association, deserve our hearty cooperation. The earnest workers who so nobly and lovingly give their lives to promote the welfare of others, give far more than though they had simply made gifts of money, so those who cannot afford to give largely need not feel discouraged on that account. After all, sympathy and good-will may be a greater force than wealth, and we can all extend to others a kindly feeling and courteous consideration, that will make life sweeter and better.

"Sometimes it seems to me we do not sufficiently realize the good that is done by money that is used in the different industries in giving employment to great numbers of people under the direction of clever men and women; and surely it takes more ability, perseverance and time to successfully manage such an enterprise than to merely make gifts."

HER PERSONALITY

Miss Gould's life at Tarrytown is an ideal one. She runs down to the city at frequent intervals, to attend to business affairs; but she lives at Lyndhurst. She entertains but few visitors, and in turn visits but seldom. The management of her property, to which she gives close attention, makes no inconsiderable call upon her time. "I have no time for society," she said, "and indeed I do not care for it at all; it is very well for those who like it."

Would you have an idea of her personality? "If so," replies Landis, "you will think of a good young woman in your own town, who loves her parents and her home; who is devoted to the church; who thinks of the poor on

Thanksgiving Day and Christmas; whose face is bright and manner unaffected; whose dress is elegant in its simplicity; who takes an interest in all things, from politics to religion; whom children love and day-laborers greet by reverently lifting the hat; and who, if she were graduated from a home seminary or college, would receive a bouquet from every boy in town. If you can think of such a young woman, and nearly every community has one (and ninety-nine times out of a hundred she is poor), you have a fair idea of the impression made on a plain man from a country town by Miss Gould."

Helen Miller Gould is just at the threshold of her beautiful career. What a promise is there in her life and work for the coming century?

She has pledged a Hall of Fame for the campus of the New York University, overlooking the Harlem river. It will have tablets for the names of fifty distinguished Americans; and proud will be the descendants of those whose names are inscribed thereon.

The human heart is the tablet upon which Miss Gould has inscribed her name, and her "Hall of Fame" is as broad and high as the republic itself.

IV

Philip D. Armour's Business Career

I MET Mr. Armour in the quiet of the Armour Institute, his great philanthropic school for young men and women. He was very courteous, and there was no delay. He took my hand with a firm grasp—reading with his steady gaze such of my characteristics as interested him,—and saying, at the same time, "Well, sir."

In stating my desire to learn such lessons from his business career as might be helpful to young men, I inquired whether the average American boy of to-day has equally *as good a chance to succeed in the world* as he had, when he began life.

"Every bit and better. The affairs of life are larger. There are greater things to do. There was never before such a demand for able men."

"Were the conditions surrounding your youth especially difficult?"

"No. They were those common to every small New York town in 1832. I was born at Stockbridge, in Madison county. Our family had its roots in Scotland. My father's ancestors were the Robertsons, Watsons, and McGregors of Scotland; my mother came of the Puritans, who settled in Connecticut."

"Dr. Gunsaulus says," I ventured, "that *all these streams of heredity set toward business affairs.*"

"Perhaps so. I like trading well. My father was reasonably prosperous and independent for those times. My mother had been a school-teacher. There were six boys, and of course such a household had to be managed with the strictest economy in those days. My mother thought it her duty to bring to our home some of the rigid discipline of the school-room. We were all trained to work together, and everything was done as systematically as possible."

"Had you access to any books?"

"Yes, the Bible, 'Pilgrim's Progress,' and a History of the United States."

It is said of the latter, by those closest to Mr. Armour, that it was as full of shouting Americanism as anything ever written, and that Mr. Armour's whole nature is yet colored by its stout American prejudices; also that it was read and re-read by the Armour children, though of this the great merchant did not speak.

"Were you always of *a robust constitution?*" I asked.

"Yes, sir. All our boys were. We were stout enough to be bathed in an ice-cold spring, out of doors, when at home. There were no bath tubs and warm water arrangements in those days. We had to be strong. My father was a stern Scotchman, and when he laid his plans they were carried out. When he set us boys to work, we worked. It was our mother who insisted on keeping us all at school, and who looked after our educational needs; while our father saw to it that we had plenty of good, hard work on the farm."

"How did you enjoy that sort of life?" I asked.

"Well enough, but not much more than any boy does. Boys are always more or less afraid of hard work."

The truth is, I have heard, but not from Mr. Armour, that when he attended the district school, he was as full of pranks and capers as the best; and that he traded jack-knives in summer and bob-sleds in winter. Young Armour was often to be found, in the winter, coasting down the long hill near the schoolhouse. Later, he had a brief term of schooling at the Cazenovia Seminary.

FOOTING IT TO CALIFORNIA

"When did you leave the farm for a mercantile life?" I asked.

"I was a clerk in a store in Stockbridge for two years, after I was seventeen, but was engaged with the farm more or less, and wanted to get out of that life. I was a little over seventeen years old when the California gold excitement of 1849 reached our town. Wonderful tales were told of gold already found, and the prospects for more on the Pacific coast. I brooded over the difference between tossing hay in the hot sun and digging up gold by handfuls, until one day I threw down my pitchfork and went over to the house and told mother that I had quit that kind of work.

"People with plenty of money could sail around Cape Horn in those days, but I had no money to spare, and so decided to walk across the country. That is, we were carried part of the way by rail and walked the rest. I persuaded one of the neighbor's boys, Calvin Gilbert, to go along with me, and we started.

"I provided myself with an old carpet sack into which to put my clothes. I bought a new pair of boots, and when we had gone as far as we could on canals and wagons, I bought two oxen. With these we managed for awhile, but eventually reached California afoot."

Young Armour suffered a severe illness on the journey, and was nursed by his companion Gilbert, who gathered herbs and steeped them for his friend's use, and once rode thirty miles in the rain to get a doctor. When they reached California, he fell in with Edward Croarkin, a miner, who nursed him back to health. The manner in which he remembered these men gives keen satisfaction to the friends of the great merchant.

"Did you have any money when you arrived at the gold-fields?"

"Scarcely any. I struck right out, though, and found a place where I could dig, and I struck pay dirt in a little time."

"Did you work entirely alone?"

"No. It was not long before I met Mr. Croarkin at a little mining camp called Virginia.

He had the next claim to mine, and we became partners. After a little while, he went away, but came back in a year. We then bought in together. The way we ran things was 'turn about.' Croarkin would cook one week, and I the next, and then we would have a clean-up every Sunday morning. We baked our own bread, and kept a few hens, which kept us supplied with eggs. There was a man named Chapin who had a little store in the village, and we would take our gold dust there and trade it for groceries."

THE DITCH

"Did you discover much gold?" I asked.

"Oh, I worked with pretty good success,—nothing startling. *I didn't waste much, and tried to live carefully.* I also *studied the business opportunities* around, and persuaded some of my friends to join me in buying and developing a 'ditch,'—a kind of aqueduct, to convey water to diggers and washers. That proved more profitable than digging for gold, and at the end of the year, the others sold out to me, took their earnings and went home. I stayed, and bought up several other water-powers, until, in 1856, I thought I had enough, and so I sold out and came East."

" How much had you made, altogether?"

" About four thousand dollars."

This was when Mr. Armour was twenty-four years old,—his capital for beginning to do business.

HE ENTERS THE GRAIN MARKET

" Did you return to Stockbridge?"

" A little while, but my ambition set in another direction. I had been studying the methods then used for moving the vast and growing food products of the West, such as grain and cattle, and I believed that I could improve them and make money. The idea and the field interested me and I decided to enter it.

" My standing was good, and I raised the money, and bought what was then the largest elevator in Milwaukee. This put me in contact with the movement of grain. At that time, John Plankington had been established in Milwaukee a number of years, and, in partnership with Frederick Layton, had built up a good pork-packing concern. I bought in with those gentlemen, and so came in contact with the work I liked. One of my brothers, Herman, had established himself in Chicago some time before, in the grain-commission business. I got him to turn that over to the care of another brother, Joseph, so that he might go to New York as a member of the new firm, of which I was a partner. It was important that the Milwaukee and Chicago houses should be able to ship to a house of their own in New York,—that is, to themselves. Risks were avoided in this way, and we were certain of obtaining all that the ever-changing markets could offer us."

"When did you begin to build up your Chicago interests?"

"They were really begun, before the war, by my brother Herman. When he went to New York for us, we began adding a small packing-house to the Chicago commission branch. It gradually grew with the growth of the West."

MR. ARMOUR'S ACUTE PERCEPTION OF THE COMMERCIAL CONDITIONS FOR BUILDING UP A GREAT BUSINESS

"Is there any one thing that accounts for the immense growth of the packing industry here?" I asked.

"System and the growth of the West did it. Things were changing at startling rates in those days. The West was growing fast. Its great areas of production offered good profits to men who would handle and ship the products. Railway lines were reaching out in new directions, or increasing their capacities and lowering their rates of transportation. These changes and the growth of the country made the creation of a food-gathering and delivering system necessary. Other things helped. At that time (1863), a great many could see that the war was going to terminate favorably for the Union. Farming operations had been enlarged by the war demand and war prices. The state banking system had been done away with, and we had a uniform currency, available everywhere, so that exchanges between the East and the West had become greatly simplified. Nothing more was needed than a steady watchfulness of the markets by competent men in continuous telegraphic communication with each other, and who knew the legitimate demand and supply, in order to sell all products quickly and with profit."

SYSTEM AND GOOD MEASURE

"Do you believe that system does so much?" I ventured.

"System and good measure. *Give a measure heaped full and running over, and success is certain.* That is what it means to be the intelligent servants of a great public need. We believed in thoughtfully adopting every attainable improvement, mechanical or otherwise, in the methods and appliances for handling every pound of grain or flesh. Right liberality and right economy will do everything where a public need is being served. Then, too, our

METHODS

improved all the time. There was a time when many parts of cattle were wasted, and the health of the city injured by the refuse. Now, by adopting the best known methods, nothing is wasted; and buttons, fertilizers, glue and other things are made cheaper and better for the world in general, out of material that was before a waste and a menace. I believe in finding out the truth about all things—the very latest truth or discovery,—and applying it."

"You attribute nothing to good fortune?"

"Nothing!" Certainly the word came well from a man whose energy, integrity, and business ability made more money out of a ditch than other men were making out of rich placers in the gold region.

Philip D. Armour

THE TURNING POINT

"May I ask what you consider the turning-point of your career?"

"The time when I began to save the money I earned at the gold-fields."

TRUTH

"What trait do you consider most essential in young men?"

"Truth. Let them get that. Young men talk about getting capital to work with. Let them get truth on board, and capital follows. It's easy enough to get that."

A GREAT ORATOR, AND A GREAT CHARITY

"Did you always desire to follow a commercial, rather than a professional life?"

"Not always. I have no talent in any other direction; but I should have liked to be a great orator."

Mr. Armour would say no more on this subject, but his admiration for oratory has been demonstrated in a remarkable way.

It was after a Sunday morning discourse by the splendid orator, Dr. Gunsaulus, at Plymouth

Church, Chicago, in which the latter had set forth his views on the subject of educating children, that Mr. Armour came forward and said:—

"You believe in those ideas of yours, do you?"

"I certainly do," said Dr. Gunsaulus.

"And would you carry them out if you had the opportunity?"

"I would."

"Well, sir," said Mr. Armour, "if you will give me five years of your time, I will give you the money."

"But to carry out my ideas would take a million dollars!" exclaimed Gunsaulus.

"I have made a little money in my time," returned Mr. Armour. And so the famous Armour Institute of Technology, to which its founder has already given sums aggregating $2,800,000, was associated with Mr. Armour's love of oratory.

One of his lieutenants says that Gerritt Smith, the old abolitionist, was Armour's boyhood's hero, and that to-day Mr. Armour will go far to hear a good speaker, often remarking that he would have preferred to be a great orator rather than a great capitalist.

Philip D. Armour

EASE IN HIS WORK

" There is no need to ask you," I continued, " whether you believe in constant, hard labor? "

" I should not call it hard. I believe in close application, of course, while laboring. Overwork is not necessary to success. Every man should have plenty of rest. I have."

" You must rise early to be at your office at half past seven? "

" Yes, but I go to bed early. I am not burning the candle at both ends."

The enormous energy of this man, who is too modest to discuss it, is displayed in the most normal manner. Though he sits all day at a desk which has direct cable connection with London, Liverpool, Calcutta, and other great centers of trade, with which he is in constant connection,—though he has at his hand long-distance telephone connection with New York, New Orleans, and San Francisco, and direct wires from his room to almost all parts of the world, conveying messages in short sentences upon subjects which involve the moving of vast amounts of stock and cereals, and the exchange of millions in money, he is not, seemingly, an overworked man. The great subjects to which he gives calm, undivided attention from early morning until evening, are laid aside with the ease with which one doffs his raiment, and outside of his office the cares weigh upon him no more. His mind takes up new and simpler things.

"What do you do," I inquired, "after your hard day's work,—think about it?"

"Not at all. I drive, take up home subjects, and never think of the office until I return to it."

"Your sleep is never disturbed?"

"Not at all."

A BUSINESS KING

And yet the business which this man forgets, when he gathers children about him and moves in his simple home circle, amounts in one year, to over $100,000,000 worth of food products, manufactured and distributed; the hogs killed, 1,750,000; the cattle, 1,080,000; the sheep, 625,000. Eleven thousand men are constantly employed, and the wages paid them are over $5,500,000; the railway cars owned and moving about all parts of the country, four thousand; the wagons of many kinds and of large number, drawn by seven hundred and fifty horses. The glue factory, employing seven hundred and fifty hands, makes over twelve million pounds of glue. In his private office, it is he who takes care of all the general affairs of this immense world of industry, and yet at half-past four he is done, and the whole subject is comfortably off his mind.

TRAINING YOUTH FOR BUSINESS

"Do you believe in inherited abilities, or that any boy can be taught and trained, and made a great and able man?"

"I recognize inherited ability. Some people have it, and only in a certain direction; but I think men can be taught and trained so that they become much better and more useful than they would be, otherwise. Some boys require more training and teaching than others. There is prosperity for everyone, according to his ability."

"What would you do with those who are naturally less competent than others?"

"Train them, and give them work according to their ability. I believe that life is all right, and that this difference which nature makes is all right. Everything is good, and is coming out satisfactorily, and we ought to make the most of conditions, and try to use and improve everything. The work needed is here, and everyone should set about doing it."

When asked if he thought the chances for young men as good to-day as they were when he was young. "Yes," he said, "I think so. The world is changing every day and new fields are constantly opening. We have new ideas, new inventions, new methods of manufacture, and new ways to-day everywhere. There is plenty of room for any man who can do anything well. The electrical field is a wonderful one. There are other things equally good, and the right man is never at a loss for an opportunity. Provided he has some ability and good sense to start with, is thrifty, honest and economical, there is no reason why any young man should not accumulate money and attain so called success in life."

When asked to what qualities he attributed his own success, Mr. Armour said: "I think that thrift and economy had much to do with it. I owe much to my mother's training and to a good line of Scotch ancestors, who have always been thrifty and economical. As to my business education, I never had any. I am, in fact, a good deal like Topsy, 'I just growed.'

Philip D. Armour

My success has been largely a matter of organization.

" I have always made it a point to surround myself with good men. I take them when they are young and keep them just as long as I can. Nearly all of the men I now have, have grown up with me. Many of them have worked with me for twenty years. They have started in at low wages, and have been advanced until they have reached the highest positions." Mr. Armour thinks that most men who accumulate a large amount of money, inherited the money-making instinct. The power of making and accumulating money, he says, is as much a natural gift as are those of a singer or an artist. " The germs of the power to make money must be in the mind. Take, for instance, the people we have working with us. I can get millions of good bookkeepers or accountants, but not more than one out of five hundred in all of those I have employed has made a great success as an organizer or trader."

Mr. Armour is a great believer in young men and young brains. He never discharges a man if he can possibly avoid it. If the man is not doing good work where he is, he puts him in some other department, but never discharges him if he can find him other work. He will not, however, tolerate intemperance, laziness or getting into debt. Some time ago a policeman entered his office. In answer to Mr. Armour's question, "What do you want here?" he replied: "I want to garnishee one of your men's wages for debt." "Indeed," said Mr. Armour, "and who is the man?" Asking the officer into his private room he sent for the debtor. "How long have you been in debt?" asked Mr. Armour. The clerk replied that he had been behind for twenty years and could not seem to catch up. "But you get a good salary, don't you?" "Yes, but I can't get out of debt." "But you must get out, or you must leave here," said Mr. Armour. "How much do you owe?" The clerk then gave the amount, which was less than a thousand dollars. "Well," said Mr. Armour, handing him a check, "there is enough to pay all your debts, and if I hear of you again getting into debt, you will have to leave." The clerk paid his debts and remodeled his life on a cash basis.

PROMPT TO ACT

In illustration of Mr. Armour's aptitude for doing business, and his energy, it is related that when, in 1893, local forces planned to defeat him in the grain market, and everyone was crying that at last the great Goliath had met his David, he was all energy. He had ordered immense quantities of wheat. The opposition had shrewdly secured every available place of storage, and rejoiced that the great packer, having no place to store his property, would suffer immense loss, and must capitulate. He foresaw the fray and its dangers, and, going over on Goose Island, bought property at any price, and began the construction of immense elevators. The town was placarded with the truth that anyone could get work at Armour's elevators. No one believed they could be done in time, but three shifts of men working night and day, often under the direct supervision of the millionaire, gradually forced the work ahead, and when, on the appointed day, the great grain-ships began to arrive, the opposition realized failure. The vessels began to pour the contents of their immense holds into these granaries, and the fight was over.

FORESIGHT

The foresight that sent him to New York in 1864, to sell pork, brought him back from Europe in 1893, months before the impending panic was dreamed of by other merchants. It is told of him that he called all his head men to New York, and announced to them:—

"Gentlemen, there's going to be financial trouble soon."

"Why, Mr. Armour," they said, "you must be mistaken. Things were never better. You have been ill, and are suddenly apprehensive."

"Oh, no," he said, "I'm not. There is going to be trouble;" and he gave as his reasons certain conditions which existed in nearly all countries, which none of those present had thought of. "Now," said he to the first of his many lieutenants, "how much will you need to run your department until next year?"

The head man named his need. The others were asked, each in turn, the same question, and, when all were through, he counted up, and, turning to the company, said:—

"Gentlemen, go back and borrow all you need in Chicago, on my credit. Use my name for all it will bring in the way of loans."

FOREARMED AGAINST PANIC

The lieutenants returned, and the name of Armour was strained to its utmost limit. When all had been borrowed, the financial flurry suddenly loomed up, but it did not worry the great packer. In his vaults were $8,000,000 in gold. All who had loaned him at interest then hurried to his doors, fearing that he also was imperiled. They found him supplied with ready money, and able to compel them to wait until the stipulated time of payment, or to force them to abandon their claims of interest for their money, and so tide him over the unhappy period. It was a master stroke, and made the name of the great packer a power in the world of finance.

SOME SECRETS OF SUCCESS

"Do you consider your financial decisions which you make quickly to be brilliant intuitions?" I asked.

"I never did anything worth doing by accident, nor did anything I have come that way. No, I never decide anything without knowing the conditions of the market, and never begin unless satisfied concerning the conclusion."

"Not everyone could do that," I said.

"I cannot do everything. Every man can do something, and there is plenty to do,—never more than now. The problems to be solved are greater now than ever before. *Never was there more need of able men. I am looking for trained men all the time.* More money is being offered for them everywhere than formerly."

"Do you consider that *happiness* consists in labor alone?"

"*It consists in doing something for others.* If you give the world better material, better measure, better opportunities for living respectably, there is happiness in that. You cannot give the world anything without labor, and there is no satisfaction in anything but such labor as looks toward doing this, and does it."

V

What Miss Mary E. Proctor Did to Popularize Astronomy

"YOU can never know what your possibilities are," said Miss Proctor, "till you have put yourself to the test. There are many, many women who long to do something, and could succeed, if they would only banish their doubts, and plunge in. For example, I was not at all sure that I could interest audiences with talks on astronomy, but, in 1893, I began, and since then have given between four and five hundred lectures."

Miss Proctor is so busy spreading knowledge of the beauties and marvels of the heavens, that she was at home in New York for only a two days' interval between tours, when she consented to talk to me about her work. This talk showed such enthusiasm and whole-souled devotion to the theme that it is easy to understand Miss Proctor's success as a lecturer, although she is physically diminutive, and is very domestic in her tastes.

AUDIENCES ARE APPRECIATIVE

"I am always nervous in going before an audience," she said, "but there is so much I want to tell them that I have no time at all to think of myself. I find that if the lecturer is really interested in the subject, those who come to listen usually are; and it is certainly true, as I have learned by going upon the platform, tired out from a long journey, that you cannot expect enthusiasm in your audience, unless you are enthusiastic yourself. But I think that audiences are very responsive and appreciative of intelligent efforts to interest them, and, therefore, I am sure, that if a woman possesses, or can acquire a thorough knowledge of some practical, popular subject, and has enthusiasm and a fair knowledge of human nature, she can attain success on the lecture platform.

"The field is broad, and far from overcrowded, and it yields bountifully to those who are willing to toil and wait. There is Miss Roberts, for instance, who commands large audiences for her lectures on music; and Mrs. Lemcke, who has been remarkably successful in her practical talks on cooking; and Mary E. Booth, who gives wonderfully instructive and entertaining lectures on the revelations of the microscope; and Miss Very, who takes audiences of children on most delightful and profitable imaginary trips to places of importance.

LECTURES TO CHILDREN

"Children, by the way, are my most satisfactory audiences. Grown-up people never become so absorbed. It is the greatest pleasure of my lecturing to talk to the little tots, and watch them drink it all in. Indeed, I prepared my very first lecture for children, but didn't deliver it. That episode marked the beginning of my career as a lecturer.

"Do you ask me to tell you about it? My father, Richard A. Proctor, wrote, as you know, many books on popular astronomy. When I was a girl I did not read them very carefully; my education at South Kensington, London, following a musical and artistic direction. In fact, I was ambitious to become a painter. But when my father died, in 1888, I found comfort in reading his books all over again; and as he had drilled me to write for his periodical,

Knowledge,' I began to write articles on astronomy for anyone who would accept them. One day, in the spring of 1893, I received a letter from Mrs. Potter Palmer, asking me if I would talk to an audience of children in the Children's Building at the World's Fair. The idea of lecturing was new to me, but I decided that I would try, at any rate, and so I took great pains to prepare a talk that I thought the children would understand, and be interested in. But when I reached the building, I found an audience, not of children, but of men and women. *There was hardly a child in all the assembled five hundred people.* It would never do to give them the childish talk I had prepared, and as it was my first attempt to talk from a platform, you can imagine my state of mind. I was determined, however, that my first effort should not be a fiasco, so I stepped out upon the platform and talked about the things that had most interested me in my father's books and conversations.

A LESSON IN LECTURING

"I have lectured a great many times since then, but my first lecture was the most trying. I am now glad that things happened as they did, for that experience taught me a valuable lesson. I learned not to commit my talks to memory, but merely to have the topics and facts and general arrangement of the lecture well in mind. By this method, I can change and adapt myself to my audience at any time; and I often have to do this. I am able to feel intuitively whether I have gained my listeners' sympathy and interest, and when I feel that I have not, I immediately take another tack. Another great advantage of not committing what you are going to say to memory, word for word, is the added color and animation and spontaneity which the conversational tone and manner gives the lecture.

THE STEREOPTICON

"My stereopticon pictures of the heavenly bodies are of great help to me. They naturally add much to the interest, and are really a revelation to most of my audiences, for the reason that they show things that can never be seen with the naked eye. How my father would have delighted in them, and how effectively he would have used them. But celestial photography had not been made practical at the time of his death; it is, indeed, quite a new art, although its general principles are very simple. A special lens and photographic plate are adjusted in the telescope, and the plate is exposed as in an ordinary camera, except that the exposure is much longer. It usually continues for about four hours, the greater the length of time the greater being the number of stars that will be seen in the photograph. After the developing, these stars appear as mere specks on the plate. That they are so small is not surprising, for most of them are stars that are never seen by the eye alone. When the photograph is enlarged by the stereopticon, the result is like looking at a considerable portion of the heavens through a powerful telescope.

"The children utter exclamations of delight when they see the pictures,—the children, dear, imaginative little souls, it is my ambition to devote more and more of my time to them, and finally talk and write for them altogether. They are greatly impressed with the new world in the skies which is opened to them, and I like to think that these early impressions will give them an understanding and appreciation of the wonders of astronomy that will always be a pleasure to them.

Miss Mary E. Proctor

"STORIES FROM STAR LAND"

"For the children, my first book, 'Stories From Star-land,' was written. I tried to weave into it poetical and romantic ideas, that appeal to the imaginative mind of the child, and quicken the interest without any sacrifice of accuracy in the facts with which I deal. I wrote the book in a week. The publisher came to me one Saturday, and told me that he would like a children's book on astronomy. I devoted all my days to it till the following Saturday night, and on Monday morning took the completed manuscript to the publishing house. They seemed very much surprised that it should be finished so soon; but as a matter of fact it was not much more than the manual labor of writing out the manuscript that I did in that week. *The little book itself is the result of ten years' thought and study.*

"It is much the same with my lectures. I deliver them in a hasty, conversational tone, and they seem, as one of my listeners told me recently, to be 'just offhand chats.' But in reality I devote a great deal of labor to them, and am constantly adding new facts and new ideas.

CONCENTRATION OF ATTENTION

"I learned very soon after I began my work, that *I must give myself up to it absolutely* if I were to achieve success. There could be no side issues, nothing else to absorb any of my energy, or take any of my thought or time. One of the first things I did was to take a thorough course in singing, for the purpose of acquiring complete control of my voice. I put aside all social functions, of which I am rather fond and have since devoted my days and nights to astronomy,—not that I work at night, except when I lecture; I rest and retire early, so that in the morning I may have the spirit and enthusiasm necessary to do good work.

"*Enthusiasm,* it seems to me, is an important factor in success. It combats discouragement, makes work a pleasure, and sacrifices easier.

"A great many women fail in special fields of endeavor, who might succeed if they were willing to sacrifice something, and would not let the distractions creep in. There is more in a woman's life to divert her attention from a single purpose than in a man's; but if the woman has chosen some line of effort that is worthy to be called life work, and if—refusing to be drawn aside,—she keeps her eyes steadfastly upon the goal, I believe that she is almost certain to achieve success. "

VI

The Boyhood Experience of President Schurman of Cornell University

AT ten years of age, he was a country lad on a backwoods farm on Prince Edward Island.

At thirteen, he had become a clerk in a country store, at a salary of thirty dollars a year.

At eighteen, he was a college student, supporting himself by working in the evenings as a bookkeeper.

At twenty, he had won a scholarship in the University of London, in competition with all other Canadian students.

At twenty-five, he was professor of philosophy, Acadia College, Nova Scotia.

At thirty-eight, he was appointed President of Cornell University.

At forty-four, he was chairman of President

McKinley's special commission to the Philippines.

In this summary is epitomized the career of Jacob Gould Schurman. It is a romance of real life such as is not unfamiliar in America. Mr. Schurman's career differs from that of some other self-made men, however. Instead of heaping up millions upon millions, he has applied his talents to winning the intellectual prizes of life, and has made his way, unaided, to the front rank of the leaders in thought and learning in this country. His career is a source of inspiration to all poor boys who have their own way to make in the world, for he has won his present honors by his own unaided efforts.

President Schurman says of his early life:—

"It is impossible for the boy of to-day, no matter in what part of the country he is brought up, to appreciate the life of Prince Edward Island as it was forty years ago. At that time, it had neither railroads nor daily newspapers, nor any of the dozen other things that are the merest commonplaces nowadays, even to the boys of the country districts. I did not see a railroad until late in my 'teens I was never inside of a theatre until after I was twenty. The only newspaper that came to my father's house was a little provincial weekly. The only books the house contained were a few standard works,—such as the Bible, Bunyan's 'Pilgrim's Progress,' Fox's 'Book of Martyrs,' and a few others of that class. Remember, too, that this was not back at the beginning of the century, but little more than a generation ago, for I was born in the year 1854.

"My father had cleared away the land on which our house stood. He was a poor man, but no poorer than his neighbors. No amount of land, and no amount of work could yield much more than the necessaries of life in that time and place. There were eight children in our family, and there was work for all of us.

A LONG TRAMP TO SCHOOL

"Our parents were anxious to have their children acquire at least an elementary education; and so, summer and winter, we tramped the mile and a half that lay between our house and the district school, and the snow often fell to the depth of five or six feet on the island, and sometimes, when it was at its worst, our father would drive us all to school in a big sleigh. But no weather was bad enough to keep us away.

"That would be looked upon as a poor kind of school, nowadays, I suppose. The scholars were of all ages, and everything, from A,-B,-C, to the Rule of Three, was taught by the one teacher. But whatever may have been its deficiencies, the work of the school was thorough. The teacher was an old-fashioned drillmaster, and whatever he drove into our heads he put there to stay. I went to this school until I was thirteen, and by that time I had learned to read and write and spell and figure with considerable accuracy.

"At the age of thirteen, I left home. I had formed no definite plans for the future. I merely wanted to get into a village, and to earn some money.

"My father got me a place in the nearest town,—Summerside,—a village of about one thousand inhabitants. For my first year's work I was to receive thirty dollars and my board. Think of that, young men of to-day! Thirty dollars a year for working from seven in the morning until ten at night! But I was glad to get the place. It was a start in the world, and the little village was like a city to my country eyes.

HE ALWAYS SUPPORTED HIMSELF

"From the time I began working in the store until to-day, I have always supported myself, and during all the years of my boyhood I never received a penny that I did not earn myself. At the end of my first year, I went to a larger store in the same town, where I was to receive sixty dollars a year and my board. I kept this place for two years, and then I gave it up, against the wishes of my employer, because I had made up my mind that I wanted to get a better education. I determined to go to college.

"I did not know how I was going to do this, except that it must be by my own efforts. I had saved about eighty dollars from my storekeeping, and that was all the money I had in the world." *Out of a hundred and fifty dollars, the only cash he received as his first earnings during three years, young Schurman had saved eighty dollars; this he invested in the beginnings of an education.*

"When I told my employer of my plan, he tried to dissuade me from it. He pointed out the difficulties in the way of my going to college, and offered to double my pay if I would stay in the store.

THE TURNING-POINT OF HIS LIFE

"That was the turning-point in my life. On one side was the certainty of one hundred and twenty dollars a year, and the prospect of promotion as fast as I deserved it. Remember what one hundred and twenty dollars meant in Prince Edward Island, and to a poor boy who had never possessed such a sum in his life. On the other side was my hope of obtaining an education. I knew that it involved hard work and self-denial, and there was the possibility of failure in the end. But my mind was made up. I would not turn back. I need not say that I do not regret that early decision, although I think that I should have made a successful storekeeper.

"With my eighty dollars capital, I began to attend the village high school, to get my preparation for college. I had only one year to do it in. My money would not last longer than that. I recited in Latin, Greek and algebra, all on the same day, and for the next forty weeks I studied harder than I ever had before or have since. At the end of the year I entered the competitive examination for a scholarship in Prince of Wales College, at Charlotte Town, on the island. I had small hope of winning it, my preparation had been so hasty and incomplete. But when the result was announced, I found that I had not only won the scholarship from my county, but stood first of all the competitors on the island.

"The scholarship I had won amounted to only sixty dollars a year. It seems little enough, but I can say now, after nearly thirty years, that the winning of it was the greatest success I have ever had. I have had other rewards, which, to most persons, would seem immeasurably greater, but with this difference: that first success was essential; without it I could not have gone on. The others I could have done without, if it had been necessary."

For two years young Schurman attended Prince of Wales College. He lived on his scholarship and what he could earn by keeping books for one of the town storekeepers, spending less than one hundred dollars during the entire college year. Afterwards, he taught a country school for a year, and then went to Acadia College in Nova Scotia to complete his college course.

Jacob Gould Schurman

A SPLENDID COLLEGE RECORD

One of Mr. Schurman's fellow-students in Acadia says that he was remarkable chiefly for taking every prize to which he was eligible. In his senior year, he learned of a scholarship in the University of London, to be competed for by the students of Canadian colleges. The scholarship paid five hundred dollars a year for three years. The young student in Acadia was ambitious to continue his studies in England, and saw in this offer his opportunity. He tried the examination and won the prize.

During the three years in the University of London, Mr. Schurman became deeply interested in the study of philosophy, and decided that he had found in it his life work. He was eager to go to Germany and study under the great leaders of philosophic thought. A way was opened for him, through the offer of the Hibbard Society in London; the prize being a traveling fellowship with two thousand dollars a year. The honor men of the great English universities like Oxford and Cambridge were among the competitors, but the poor country boy from Prince Edward Island was again successful, greatly to the surprise of the others.

At the end of his course in Germany, Mr. Schurman, then a Doctor of Philosophy, returned to Acadia College to become a teacher there. Soon afterwards, he was called to Dalhousie University, at Halifax, Nova Scotia. In 1886, when a chair of philosophy was established at Cornell, President White, who once met the brilliant young Canadian, called him to that position. Two years later, Dr. Schurman became Dean of the Sage School of Philosophy at Cornell; and, in 1892, when the President's chair became vacant, he was placed at the head of the great university. At that time, he was only thirty-eight years of age.

President Schurman is a man of great intellectual power, and an inspiring presence. Though one of the youngest college presidents in the country, he is one of the most successful, and under his leadership Cornell has been very prosperous. He is deeply interested in all the affairs of young men, and especially those who, as he did, must make their own way in the world. He said, the other day:—

"Though I am no longer engaged directly in teaching, I should think my work a failure if I did not feel that my influence on the young men with whom I come in contact is as direct and helpful as that of a teacher could be."

VII

The Story of John Wanamaker

IN a plain two-story dwelling, on the outskirts of Philadelphia, the future merchant prince was born, July 11, 1837. His parents were Americans in humble station; his mother being of that sturdy Pennsylvania Dutch stock which has no parallel except the Scotch for ruggedness. His father, a hard-working man, owned a brickyard in the close vicinity of the family residence. Little John earned his first money, seven big copper cents, by assisting his father. He was too small to do much, but turned the bricks every morning as they lay drying in the summer sun. As he grew older and stronger, the boy was given harder tasks around the brickyard.

He went to school a little, not much, and he assisted his mother in the house a great deal. His father died when John was fourteen, and this changed the whole course of his life. He abandoned the brickyard and secured a place in a bookstore owned by Barclay Lippincott, on Market Street, Philadelphia, at a salary of one dollar and twenty-five cents a week.

It was a four-mile walk from his home to his place of business. Cheerfully he trudged this distance morning and night; purchasing an apple or a roll each noon for luncheon, and giving his mother all the money that he saved. He used to deny himself every comfort, and the only other money that he ever spent was on books for his mother. This seems to have been the boy's chief source of pleasure at that period. Even to-day, he says of his mother: "Her smile was a bit of heaven, and it never faded out of her face till her dying day." Mrs. Wanamaker lived to see her son famous and wealthy.

HIS CAPITAL AT FOURTEEN

John Wanamaker, the boy, had no single thing in all his surroundings to give him an advantage over any one of hundreds of other boys in the city of Philadelphia. Indeed, there were hundreds and hundreds of other boys of his own age for whom anyone would have felt safe in prophesying a more notable career. His capital was not in money. Very few boys in all that great city had less money than John Wanamaker, and comparatively few families of average position but were better off in the way of worldly goods. John Wanamaker's capital, that stood him in such good stead in after life, comprised good health, good habits, a clean mind, thrift in money matters, and tireless devotion to whatever he thought to be duty.

People who were well acquainted with John Wanamaker when he was a book publisher's boy, say that he was exceptionally promising as a boy; that he was studious as well as attentive to business. He did not take kindly to rough play, or do much playing of any kind. He was earnest in his work, unusually earnest for a boy. And he was saving of his money.

When, a little later, he went to a Market street clothing house and asked for a place, he had no difficulty in getting it, nor had he any trouble in holding it, and here he could earn twenty-five cents a week more wages.

TOWER HALL CLOTHING STORE

Men who worked with him in the Tower Hall Clothing Store say that he was always bright, willing, accommodating, and very seldom out of temper. His effort was to be first at the store in the morning, and he was very likely to be one of the last, if not the last, at the store in the evening. If there was an errand, he was always prompt and glad to do it. And so the store people liked him, and the proprietor liked him, and, when he began to sell clothing, the customers liked him. He was considerate of their interests. He did not try to force undesirable goods upon them. He treated them so that when they came again they would be apt to ask, "Where is John?"

HIS AMBITION AND POWER AS AN ORGANIZER AT SIXTEEN

Colonel Bennett, the proprietor of Tower Hall, said of him at this time:—

"John was certainly the most ambitious boy I ever saw. I used to take him to lunch with me, and he used to tell me how he was going to be a great merchant.

"He was very much interested in the temperance cause; and had not been with me long before he persuaded most of the employees in the store to join the temperance society to which he belonged. He was always organizing something. He seemed to be a natural-born organizer. This faculty is largely accountable for his great success in after life."

THE Y. M. C. A.

Young Wanamaker's religious principles were always at the forefront in whatever he did. His interest in Sunday School work, and his skill as an organizer became well known. And so earnestly did he engage in the work of the Young Men's Christian Association, that he was appointed the first salaried secretary of the Philadelphia branch, at one thousand dollars a year. Never since has a secretary enrolled so many members in the same space of time. He passed seven years in this arduous work.

OAK HALL

He saved his money; and, at twenty-four, formed a partnership with his brother-in-law Nathan Brown, and opened Oak Hall Clothing store, in April, 1861. Their united capital was only $3,500; yet Wanamaker's capital of popular good-will was very great. He was already a great power in the city. I can never forget the impression made upon my mind, after he had been in business but a few months, when I visited his Bethany Sunday School, established in one of the most unpromising sections of the city, which had become already a factor for good, with one of the largest enrollments in the world. And he was foremost in every form of philanthropic work.

It was because of his great capacity to do business that Wanamaker had been able to "boom" the Young Men's Christian Association work. He knew how to do it. And he could "boom" a Sunday School, or anything else that he took hold of. He had

A HEAD BUILT FOR BUSINESS,

whatever the business might be. And as for Oak Hall, he knew just what to do with it.

The first thing he did was to multiply his working capital by getting the best help obtainable for running the store.

At the very outset, John Wanamaker did what almost any other business man would have stood aghast at. He chose the best man he knew as a salesman in the clothing business in Philadelphia,—the man of the most winning personality who could attract trade,—and agreed to pay him $1,350 for a year,—one-third of the entire capital of the new concern.

It has been a prime principle with this merchant prince not only to deal fairly with his employees, but to make it an object for them to earn money for him and to stand by him. Capacity has been the first demand. *He engaged the very best men to be had.* There are to-day dozens of men in his employ who receive larger salaries than are paid to cabinet ministers. All the employees of the Thirteenth Street store, which he occupied in 1877, participate in *a yearly division of profits. Their share at the end of the first year amounted to* $109,439.68.

HIS RELATION TO CUSTOMERS

A considerable portion of the trade of the new store came from people in the country districts. Mr. Wanamaker had a way of getting close to them and gaining their good will. He understood human nature. He put his customer at ease. He showed interest in the things that interested the farmer. An old employee of the firm says: "John used to put a lot of chestnuts in his pocket along in the fall and winter, and, when he had one of these countrymen in tow, he'd slip a few of the nuts into the visitor's hand and both would go munching about the store."

Wanamaker was the first to introduce the "one-price system" into the clothing trade. It was the universal rule in those days, in the clothing trade, not to mark the prices plainly on the goods that were for sale. Within rather liberal bounds, the salesman got what he could from the customer. Mr. Wanamaker, after a time, instituted at Oak Hall the plan of "but one price and that plainly marked." In doing this he followed the cue of Stewart, who was the first merchant in the country to introduce it into the dry-goods business.

The great Wanamaker store of 1877 went much further:—

He announced that *those who bought goods of him were to be satisfied with what they bought, or have their money back.*

To the old mercantile houses of the city, this seemed like committing business suicide.

It was, also, unheard-of that special effort should be made to add to the comfort of visitors; to make them welcome whether they cared to buy or not; to induce them to look upon the store as a meeting-place, a rendezvous, a resting-place,—a sort of city home, almost.

THE MERCHANT'S ORGANIZING FACULTY

was so great that General Grant once remarked to George W. Childs that Wanamaker would have been a great general if his lot had been that of army service.

Wanamaker used to buy goods of Stewart, and the New York merchant remarked to a friend: "If young Wanamaker lives, he will be a greater merchant than I ever was."

Sometime in recent years, since Wanamaker bought the Stewart store, he said to Frank G. Carpenter:—

"A. T. Stewart was a genius. I have been surprised again and again as I have gone through the Broadway and Tenth Street building, to find what a knowledge he had of the needs of a mercantile establishment. Mr. Stewart put up a building which is to-day, I believe, better arranged than any of the modern structures. He seemed to know just what was needed.

"I met him often when I was a young man. I have reason to think that he took a liking to me. One day, I remember, I was in his woolen department buying some stuffs for my store here, when he came up to me and asked if I would be in the store for fifteen minutes longer. I replied that I would. At the end of fifteen minutes he returned and handed me a slip of paper, saying:—

"'Young man, I understand that you have a mission school in Philadelphia; use that for it.'

"Before I could reply he had left. I looked down at the slip of paper. It was a check for one thousand dollars."

Wanamaker early showed himself the peer of the greatest merchants. He created the combination or department store. He lifted the retail clothing business to a higher plane than it had ever before reached. In ten years from the time he began to do business for himself, he had absorbed the space of forty-five other tenants and become the leading merchant of his native city. Four years later, he had purchased, for $450,000, the freight depot of the Pennsylvania Railroad, covering the entire square where his present great store is located. The firm name became simply John Wanamaker. His lieutenants and business partners therein are his son Thomas B. Wanamaker, and Robert C. Ogden. Their two Philadelphia establishments alone do a business of between

$30,000,000 and $40,000,000 annually. Mr. Wanamaker's private fortune is one of the most substantial in America.

ATTENTION TO DETAILS

Yet in all these years he has been early and late at the store, as he was when a boy. He has always seen to it that customers have prompt and careful attention. He early made the rule that if a sale was missed, a written reason must be rendered by the salesman. There was no hap-hazard business in that store,—nothing of the happy-go-lucky style. Each man must be alert, wide-awake, attentive, or there was no place for him at Oak Hall.

THE MOST RIGID ECONOMY

has been always a part of the system. It is told of him that, in the earlier days of Oak Hall, he used to gather up the short pieces of string that came in on parcels, make them into a bunch, and see that they were used when bundles were to be tied. He also had a habit of smoothing out old newspapers, and seeing that they were used as wrappers for such things as did not require a better grade of paper.

The story has been often related of the first

day's business at the original store in '61, when Wanamaker delivered the sales by wheeling a push-cart.

ADVERTISING

The first day's business made a cash profit of thirty-eight dollars; and the whole sum was invested in one advertisement in the next day's "*Inquirer.*"

His advertising methods were unique; he paid for the best talent he could get in this line.

Philadelphia woke one morning to find "W. & B." in the form of six-inch square posters stuck up all over the town. There was not another letter, no hint, just "W. & B." Such things are common enough now, but then the whole city was soon talking and wondering what this sign meant. After a few days, a second poster modestly stated that Wanamaker & Brown had begun to sell clothing at Oak Hall. Before long there were great signs, each 100 feet in length, painted on special fences built in a dozen places about the city, particularly near the railroad stations. These told of the new firm and were the first of a class that is now seen all over the country. Afterwards

BALLOONS

more than twenty feet high were sent up, and a suit of clothes was given to each person who brought one of them back. Whole counties were stirred up by the balloons. It was grand advertising, imitated since by all sorts of people. When the balloon idea struck the Oak Hall management it was quickly found that the only way to get these air-ships was to make them, and so, on the roof of the store, the cotton cloth was cut and oiled and put together. Being well built, and tied very tightly at the neck, they made long flights and some of them were used over and over again. In one instance, a balloon remained for more than six months in a cranberry swamp, and when the great bag was discovered, slowly swaying in the breeze, among the bushes, the frightened Jerseymen thought they had come upon an elephant, or, maybe, a survivor of the mastodons. This made more advertising of the very best kind for the clothing store,—the kind that excites interested, complimentary talk.

SEIZING OPPORTUNITIES

Genius consists in taking advantage of opportunities quite as much as in making them. Here was a young man doing things in an advertising way regardless of the custom of the business world, and with a wonderful knowledge of human nature. He took common-sense advantage of opportunities that were open to everybody.

Soon after the balloon experience, tally-ho coaching began to be a Philadelphia fad of the very exclusives. Immediately afterwards a crack coach was secured, and six large and spirited horses were used instead of four, and Oak Hall employees, dressed in the style of the most ultra coaching set, traversed the country in every direction, scattering advertising matter to the music of the horn. Sometimes they would be a week on a trip. No wonder Oak Hall flourished. It was kept in the very front of the procession all the time.

A little later, in the yachting season, the whole town was attracted and amused by processions and scatterings of men, each wearing a wire body frame that supported a thin staff from which waved a wooden burgee, or pointed flag reminding them of Oak Hall. Nearly two hundred of these prototypes of the "Sandwich man" were often out at one time.

But it was not only in the quick catching of a novel advertising thought that the new house was making history; in newspaper advertising, it was even urther in advance. The statements of store nev s were crisp and unhackneyed, and the first ar istic illustrations ever put into advertisemenes were used there. So high was the grade of this picture-work that art schools regularly clipped the illustrations as models; and the world-famous Shakespearian scholar, Dr. Horace Howard Furness, treasured the original sketches of "The Seven Ages" as among the most interesting in his unique collection.

PUSH AND PERSISTENCE

"The chief reason," said Mr. Wanamaker upon one occasion, "that everybody is not successful is the fact that they have not enough persistency. I always advise young men who write me on the subject to do one thing well, throwing all their energies into it."

To his employees he once said:—"We are very foolish people if we shut our ears and eyes to what other people are doing. I often pick up things from strangers. As you go along, pick up suggestions here and there, jot them down and send them along. Even writing them down helps to concentrate your mind on that part of the work. You need not be afraid of overstepping the mark. The more we push each other, the better."

"TO WHAT, MR. WANAMAKER, DO YOU ATTRIBUTE YOUR GREAT SUCCESS?"

In reply to this question when asked, he replied:—"To thinking, toiling, trying, and trusting in God."

A serene confidence in a guiding power has always been one of the Wanamaker characteristics. He is always calm. Under the greatest stress he never loses his head.

In one physical particular, Mr. Wanamaker is very remarkable. He can work continually for a long time without sleep and without evidence of strain, and make up for it by a good rest afterwards.

When upon one occasion he was asked to name the essentials of success, he replied, curtly:—"I might write a volume trying to tell you how to succeed. *One way is to not be above taking a hint from a master.* I don't care to tell why I succeeded; because I object to talking about myself,—it isn't modest."

A feature of his make-up that has contributed largely to his success is his ability to concentrate his thoughts. No matter how trivial the subject brought before him, he takes it up with the appearance of one who has nothing else on his mind.

HIS VIEWS ON BUSINESS

When asked whether the small tradesmen has any "show" to-day against the great department stores, he said:—

"All of the great stores were small at one time. Small stores will keep on developing into big ones. You wouldn't expect a man to put an iron band about his business in order to prevent expansion, would you? There are, according to statistics, a greater number of prosperous small stores in the city than ever before. What better proof do you want?

"The department store is a natural product, evolved from conditions that exist as a result of fixed trade laws. Executive capacity, combined with command of capital, finds opportunity in these conditions, which are harmonious with the irresistible determination of the producer to meet the consumer directly, and of merchandise to find distribution along the lines of least resistance. Reduced prices stimulate consumption, and increase employment; and it is sound opinion that the increased employment created by the department stores goes to women without curtailing that of men. In general it may be stated that large retail stores have shortened the hours of labor; and by systematic discipline have made it lighter. The small store is harder upon the sales-person and clerk. The effects upon the character and capacity of the employees are good. A well ordered, modern retail store is the means of education in spelling, writing, English language, system and method. Thus it becomes to the ambitious and serious employees, in a small way, a university, in which character is broadened by intelligent instruction practically applied."

When asked if a man with means but no experience would be safe in embarking in a mercantile business, he replied quickly:—

"A man can't drive a horse who has never seen one. No; a man must have training, must know how to buy and sell; only experience teaches that."

I have heard people marvel at the unbroken upward course of Mr. Wanamaker's career, and lament that they so often make mistakes. But hear him:—

"Who does not make mistakes? Why, if I were to think only of the mistakes I have made, I should be miserable indeed."

I have heard it said a hundred times that Mr. Wanamaker started when success was easy. Here is what he says himself about it:—

"I think I could succeed as well now as in the past. It seems to me that the conditions of to-day are even more favorable to success than when I was a boy. There are better facilities for doing business, and more business to be done. Information in the shape of books and newspapers is now in the reach of all, and the young man has two opportunities where he formerly had one.

"We are much more afraid of combinations of capital than we have any reason for being. Competition regulates everything of that kind. No organization can make immense profits for any length of time without its field soon swarming with competitors. It requires brain and muscle to manage any kind of business, and the same elements which have produced business success in the past will produce it now, and will always produce it."

PUBLIC SERVICE

With the exception of his term of service as postmaster-general of the United States in President Harrison's cabinet—a service which was marked by great executive ability and the institution of many reforms,—Mr. Wanamaker has devoted his attention almost entirely to his business and his church work.

Yet as a citizen he has always taken a most positive course in opposition to the evils that threaten society. He has been forever prompted by his religious convictions to pursue vice either in the "dive," or in municipal, state or national life. He hates a barroom, but he hates a treasury looter far more fiercely. His idea of Christian duty was evidently derived from the scene wherein the Master took a scourge and drove the corrupt traders and office-holders out of the temple. It is vigorous, it is militant; but it makes enemies. Consequently, Mr. Wanamaker is not without persistent maligners; getting himself well hated by the worst men in the community.

INVEST IN YOURSELF

Mr. Wanamaker's views of what life is for

are well expressed in the following excerpt from one of his addresses to young men.

In the course of his address, he related that he was once called upon to invest in an expedition to recover Spanish mahogany and doubloons from the Spanish Main, which, for half a century, had lain under the rolling waves in sunken frigates. "But, young men," he continued, "I know of better expeditions than this right at home, deep down under the sea of neglect and ignorance and discouragement. Near your own feet lie treasures untold, and you can have them all for your own by earnest watch and faithful study and proper care.

"Let us not be content to mine the most coal, make the largest locomotives and weave the largest quantities of carpets; but, amid the sounds of the pick, the blows of the hammer, the rattle of the looms, and the roar of the machinery, take care that the immortal mechanism of God's own hand,—the mind,—is still full-trained for the highest and noblest service.

"This is the most enduring kind of property to acquire, a property of soul which no disaster can wreck or ruin. Whatever may be the changes that shall sweep over our fair land, no power can ever take away from you your investments in knowledge."

AT HOME

Like all other magnetic and forceful men, Mr. Wanamaker is striking in appearance, strong rather than handsome. He has a full, round head, a broad forehead, a strong nose, heavy-lidded eyes that flash with energy, heavy jaws that denote strength of will, and tightly closed lips that just droop at the corners, giving an ever-present touch of sedateness. His face is as smooth as a boy's and as mobile as an actor's; and, when lighted up in discussion, it beams with expression. He wears a hat that is only six and seven-eighths in size, but is almost completely circular in form. He is almost six feet tall and finely built, and all his motions have in them the springiness of health. Nobody ever saw him dressed in any other color than black, with a black necktie under a "turn-down" collar. But he always looks as trim as if he were just out of the hands of both tailor and barber.

It is his delight to pass much time at his country seat in Jenkintown. He is fond of the field and the river, the trees and flowers, and all the growths with which God has beautified the earth. His house is a home-like structure, with wide piazzas, standing upon the crest of a hill in the midst of a noble lawn. A big rosery and orchid house stand near by. The before-breakfast ramble of the proprietor is finished in the flower garden, and every guest is laden with floral trophies.

Mr. Wanamaker was married, while he was the Secretary of the Y. M. C. A., to one whom he met at a church service, and who has been in full sympathy with his religious activities. He has been for forty years superintendent of the Bethany Sunday School in Philadelphia. He began with two teachers and twenty-seven pupils; and at the recent anniversary reported a school of 4,500, a church with 3,700 members, 500 having been added during the past year, several branches, and scores of department organizations.

John Wanamaker says to-day that his business success is due to his religious training. He is first of all a Christian.

The lesson of such a life should be precious to every young man. It teaches the value of untiring effort, of economy, of common sense applied to common business. I know of no career in this country that offers more encouragement to young people. It shows what persistency can do; it shows what intelligent, well-directed, tireless effort can do; and it proves that a man may devote himself to helping others, to the Sunday School, to the Church, to broad philanthropy, and still be wonderfully successful in a business way.

VIII

Giving up Five Thousand Dollars a Year to Become a Sculptor

"MY life?" queried F. Wellington Ruckstuhl, one of the foremost sculptors of America, as we sat in his studio looking up at his huge figure of "Force." "When did I begin to sculpture? As a child I was forever whittling, but I did not have dreams then of becoming a sculptor. It was not till I was thirty-two years of age. And love,—disappointment in my first love played a prominent part."

"But as a boy, Mr. Ruckstuhl?"

"I was a poet. Every sculptor or artist is necessarily a poet. I was always reaching out and seeking the beautiful. My father was a foreman in a St. Louis machine shop. He came to this country in a sailing ship from

Alsace, by way of the Gulf to St. Louis, when I was but six years old. He was a very pious man and a deacon in a church. One time, Moody and Sankey came to town, and my father made me attend the meetings; I think he hoped that I would become a minister. Between the ages of fourteen and nineteen, I worked in a photographic supply store; wrote one hundred poems, and read incessantly. I enlarged a view of the statue of Nelson in Trafalgar Square, London, into a 'plaster sketch,' ten times as large as the picture, but still I did not know my path. I began the study of philosophy, and kept up my reading for ten years. My friends thought I would become a literary man. I wrote for the papers, and belonged to a prominent literary club. I tried to analyze myself. 'I am a man,' I said, 'but what am I good for? What am I to make of this life?' I drifted from one position to another. Every one was sorry to part with my services, for I always did my duties as well as they could be done. When I was twenty-five years of age, the girl to whom I was attached was forced by her mother to marry a wealthy man. She died a year afterwards; and I 'pulled up stakes,' and started on a haphazard, reckless career. I went to Colorado, drifted into Arizona, prospected, mined, and worked on a ranch. I went to California, and at one time thought of shipping for China. My experiences would fill a book. Again I reached St. Louis. For a year, I could not find a thing to do, and became desperate."

"And you had done nothing at art so far?" I asked.

"At that time, I saw a clay sketch. I said to myself, 'I can do as well as that,' and I copied it. My second sketch admitted me to the St. Louis Sketch Club. I told my friends that I would be a sculptor. They laughed and ridiculed me. I had secured a position in a store, and at odd times worked at what I had always loved, but had only half realized it. Notices appeared in the papers about me, for I was popular in the community. I entered the competition for a statue of General Frank R. Blair. I received the first prize, but when the committee discovered that I was only a bill clerk in a store, they argued that I was not competent to carry out the work; although I was given the first prize model and the one hundred and fifty dollars accompanying it."

"But that inspired you?"

'Yes, but my father and mother put every obstacle in the way possible. I was driven from room to room. I was not even allowed to work in the attic." Here Mr. Ruckstuhl laughed. "You see what genius has to contend with. I was advanced in position in the store, till I became assistant manager, at two thousand dollars a year. When I told the proprietor that I had decided to be a sculptor, he gazed at me in blank astonishment. 'A sculptor?' he queried, incredulously, and made a few very discouraging remarks, emphasized with dashes. 'Why, young man, are you going to throw up the chance of a lifetime? I will give you five thousand dollars a year, and promote you to be manager if you will remain with me.'

"But I had found my life's work," said Mr. Ruckstuhl, turning to me. "I knew it would be a struggle through poverty, till I attained fame. But I was confident in myself, which is half of the battle."

"And you went abroad?"

"Yes, with but two hundred and fifty dollars," he replied. "I traveled through Europe for five months and visited the French

Salon. I said to myself, 'I can do that, and that;' and my confidence grew. But there was some work that completely 'beat' me. I returned to America penniless, but with a greater insight into art. I determined that I would retrace my steps to Paris, and study there for three years, and thought that would be sufficient to fully develop me. My family and friends laughed me to scorn, and I was discouraged by everyone. In four months, in St. Louis, I secured seven orders for busts, at two hundred dollars each, to be done after my return from France. That shows that some persons had confidence in me and in my talent. .

"O, the student life in Paris! How I look back with pleasure upon those struggling, yet happy days! In two months, I started on my female figure of 'Evening,' in the nude, that is now in the Metropolitan Museum of Art. I finished it in nine months, and positively sweat blood in my work. I sent it to the Salon, and went to Italy. When I returned to Paris, I saw my name in the paper with honorable mention. I suppose you can realize my feelings; I experienced the first flush of victory. I brought it to America, and exposed it in St. Louis. Strange to say, I rose in the estimation of even my family. My father actually congratulated me. A wealthy man in St. Louis gave me three thousand dollars to have my 'Evening' put into marble. I returned with it to Paris, and in a month and a quarter it was exhibited in the Salon. At the World's Fair, at Chicago, it had the place of honor, and received one of the eleven grand medals given to American sculptors. In 1892, I came to New York. This statue of 'Force' will be erected, with my statue of 'Wisdom,' on the new Court of Appeals in New York."

We gazed at it, seated, and clothed in partial armor, of the old Roman type, and holding a sword across its knees. The great muscles spoke of strength and force, and yet, with it all, there was an almost benign look upon the military visage.

"There is force and real action there withal, although there is repose." I said in admiration.

"Oh," said Mr. Ruckstuhl, "that's it, and that is what it is so hard to get! That is what every sculptor strives for; and, unless he attains it, his work, from my point of view, is worthless. There must be life in a statue; it must almost breathe. In repose there must be dormant action that speaks for itself."

"Is most of your work done under inspiration?" I asked.

"There is nothing,—and a great deal,—in so-called inspiration. I firmly believe that we mortals are merely tools, mediums, at work here on earth. I peg away, and bend all my energies to my task. I simply accomplish nothing. Suddenly, after considerable preparatory toil, the mist clears away; I see things clearly; everything is outlined for me. I believe there is a conscious and a sub-conscious mind. The sub-conscious mind is the one that does original work; it cannot be affected by the mind that is conscious to all our petty environments. When the conscious mind is lulled and silenced, the sub-conscious one begins to work. That I call inspiration."

"Are you ever discouraged?" I asked out of curiosity.

"Continually," replied Mr. Ruckstuhl, looking down at his hands, soiled with the working clay. "Some days I will be satisfied with what I have done. It will strike me as simply fine. I will be as happy as a bird, and leave simply joyous. The following morning, when the cloths are removed, I look at my previous toil, and consider it vile. I ask myself: 'Are you a sculptor or not? Do you think that you ever will be one? Do you consider that art?' So it is, till your task is accomplished. You are your own critic, and are continually distressed at your inability to create your ideals."

Mr. F. Wellington Ruckstuhl is forty-six years of age; neither short nor tall; a brilliant man, with wonderful powers of endurance, for his work is more exacting and tedious than is generally supposed.

"I have simply worked a month and a quarter on that statue," he said. "Certain work dissatisfied me, and I obliterated it. I have raised that head three times. My eyes get weary, and I become physically tired. On such occasions I sit down and smoke a little to distract my thoughts, and to clear my mind. Then my sub-conscious mind comes into play again," he concluded with a smile.

Mr. Ruckstuhl's best known works are: "Mercury Teasing the Eagle of Jupiter," which is of bronze, nine feet high, which he made in Paris; a seven-foot statue of Solon, erected in the Congressional Library, at Washington; busts of Franklin, Gœthe and Macaulay, on the front of the same library; and the eleven-foot statue of bronze of "Victory," for the Jamaica soldiers' and sailors' monument. In competition, he won the contract for an equestrian statue of General John F. Hartrauft, ex-Governor of Pennsylvania, which he also made in Paris. It is considered the finest piece of work of its kind in America. Besides this labor, he has made a number of medallions and busts; and with the completion of his statue of "Force," he will have made a wonderful record.

"Art was in me as a child," he said: "I was discouraged whenever it beckoned me, but finally claimed me. I surrendered a good position to follow it, whether it led through a thorny road or not. A sculptor is an artist, a musician, a poet, a writer, a dramatist,—to throw action, breath and life, music and a soul into his creation. I can pick up an instrument and learn it instantly; I can sing, and act, so I am in touch with the sympathies of the beings that I endeavor to create. You will find most sculptors and artists of my composite nature.

"There," said Mr. Ruckstuhl, and he stretched out his arm, with his palm downward, and moved it through the air, as he gazed into distance, "you strive to create the imagination of your mind, and it comes to you as if sent from another world."

"You strive." That is the way to success.

IX

Questions and Answers: Business Pointers by Darius Ogden Mills

"WHAT is your idea, Mr. Mills,[1] of a successful life?" "If a bootblack does all the good he possibly can for his fellow-men, his life has been just as successful as that of the millionaire who helps thousands."

WORK

"What, Mr. Mills, do you consider the keynote of success?"

"Work," he replied, quickly and emphatically. "Work develops all the good there is in a man; idleness all the evil. Work sharpens all

[1] Mr. Mills was born in Western New York in 1825. He has been a leading financier for fifty years, in California, and in New York. He is connected with the management of eighteen important business and philanthropic corporations in New York city.

his faculties and makes him thrifty; idleness makes him lazy and a spendthrift. Work surrounds a man with those whose habits are industrious and honest; in such society a weak man develops strength, and a strong man is made stronger. Idleness, on the other hand, is apt to throw a man into the company of men whose object in life is usually the pursuit of unwholesome and demoralizing diversions."

SELF-DEPENDENCE

"To what formative influence do you attribute your material success, Mr. Mills?" I asked.

"I was taught very early that I would have to depend entirely upon myself; that my future lay in my own hands. I had that for a start, and it was a good one. I didn't waste any time thinking about succession to wealth, which so often acts as a drag upon young men. Many persons waste the best years of their lives waiting for dead men's shoes; and, when they get them, find them entirely too big to wear gracefully, simply because they have not developed themselves to wear them.

"As a rule, the small inheritance, which, to a boy, would seem large, has a tendency to lessen his efforts, and is a great damage to him in the way of acquiring the habits necessary to success.

HABIT OF THRIFT

"No one can acquire a fortune unless he makes a start; and the habit of thrift, which he learns in saving his first hundred dollars, is of inestimable value later on. It is not the money, but the habit which counts.

"There is no one so helpless as a man who is 'broke,' no matter how capable he may be, and there is no habit so detrimental to his reputation among business men as that of borrowing small sums of money. This cannot be too emphatically impressed upon young men.

EXPENSIVE HABITS—SMOKING

"Another thing is that none but the wealthy, and very few of them, can afford the indulgence of expensive habits; how much less then can a man with only a few dollars in his pocket? More young men are ruined by the expense of smoking than in any other way. The money thus laid out would make them independent, in many cases, or at least would give them a good start. A young man should be warned by the melancholy example of those who have been ruined by smoke, and avoid it."

FORMING AN INDEPENDENT BUSINESS JUDGMENT

"What marked traits," Mr. Mills, "have the influential men with whom you have been associated, possessed, which most impressed you?"

"A habit of thinking and acting for themselves. No end of people are ruined by taking the advice of others. This may answer temporarily, but in the long run it is sure to be disastrous. Any man who hasn't ability to judge for himself would better get a comfortable clerkship somewhere, letting some one of more ambition and ability do the thinking necessary to run the business."

THE MULTIPLICATION OF OPPORTUNITIES TO-DAY IN AMERICA

"Are the opportunities for making money as numerous to-day as they were when you started in business?"

"Yes, the progress of science and invention has increased the opportunities a thousandfold, and a man can find them wherever he seeks them in the United States in particular. It has caused the field of employment of labor of all kinds to expand enormously, thus creating opportunities which never existed before. It is no longer necessary for a man to go to foreign countries or distant parts of his own country to make money. Opportunities come to him in every quarter. There is hardly a point in the country so obscure that it has not felt the revolutionizing influence of commercial enterprise. Probably railroads and electricity are the chief instruments in this respect. Other industries follow closely in their wake."

WHERE ONE'S BEST CHANCE IS—THE KNOWLEDGE OF MEN

"In what part of the country do you think the best chances for young men may be found?"

"The best place for a young man to make money is the town in which he was born and educated. There he learns all about everybody, and everybody learns about him. This is to his advantage if he bears a good character, and to the advantage of his towns-people if he bears a bad one. While a young man is growing up, he unconsciously absorbs a vast deal of knowledge of people and affairs, which would be equal to money if he only has the judgment to avail himself of it. A knowledge of men is the prime secret of business success. Upon reflection, how absurd it is for a man to leave a town where he knows everything and everybody, and go to some distant point where he doesn't know anything about anybody or anything, and expect to begin on an equal footing with the people there who are thoroughly acquainted."

THE BOTTOM OF THE LADDER

"What lesson," Mr. Mills, "do you consider it most needful for young men to learn?"

"The lesson of humility;—not in the sense of being servile or undignified, but in that of paying due respect to men who are their superiors in the way of experience, knowledge and position. Such a lesson is akin to that of discipline. Members of the royal families of Europe are put in subordinate positions in the navies or armies of their respective countries, in order that they may receive the training necessary to qualify them to take command. They must first know how to obey, if they would control others.

"In this country, it is customary for the sons of the presidents of great railroads, or other companies, to begin at the bottom of the ladder and work their way up step by step, just the same as any other boy in the employ of the corporation. This course has become imperatively necessary in the United States, where each great business has become a profession in itself. Most of the big machine shops number among their employees, scions of old families who carry dinner pails, and work with files or lathes, the same as anyone else. Such shoulder-to-shoulder experience is invaluable to a man who is destined to command, because he not only masters the trade technically, but learns all about the men he works with and qualifies himself to grapple with labor questions which may arise.

"There is no end of conspicuous examples of the wisdom of this system in America. There are also many instances of disaster to great industrial concerns due to the inexperience or the lack of tact of men placed suddenly in control."

THE BENEFICENT USE OF CAPITAL

Upon this point, Mr. Mills said:—"A man can, in the accumulation of a fortune, be just as great a benefactor of mankind as in the distribution of it. In organizing a great industry, one opens up fields of employment for a multitude of people who might otherwise be practically helpless, giving them not only a chance to earn a living for themselves and their families, but also to lay by a competency for old age. All honest, sober men, if they have half a chance, can do that; but only a small percentage can ever become rich. Now the rich man, having acquired his wealth, knows better how to manage it than those under him would, and having actual possession, he has the power to hold the community of his employees and their interests together, and prevent disintegration, which means disaster so much oftener to the employee than to the employer."

THE WHOLESOME DISCIPLINE OF EARNING AND SPENDING

"What is the responsibility of wealth, Mr. Mills?"

"A man must learn not to think too much of money. It should be considered as a means and not an end; and the love for it should never be permitted to so warp a man's mind as to destroy his interest in progressive ideas. Making money is an education, and the wide experience thus acquired teaches a man discrimination in both men and projects, where money is under consideration. Very few men who make their own money use it carelessly. Most good projects that fail owe their failure to bad business management, rather than to lack of intrinsic merit. An inventor may have a very good thing, and plenty of capital may be enlisted but if a man not acquainted with the peculiar line, or one who is not a good salesman or financier be employed as manager, the result is disastrous. A man should spend his money in a way that tends to advance the best interests of society in the country he lives in, or in his own neighborhood at least. There is only one thing that is a greater harm to the community than a rich spendthrift, and that is a miser."

PERSONAL: A WORD ABOUT CHEAP HOTELS

"How did you happen to establish the system of hotels which bears your name, Mr. Mills?"

"I had been looking around for several years to find something to do that would be for the good of the community. My mind was largely on other matters, but it occurred to me that the hotel project was the best, and I immediately went to work at it. My purpose was to do the work on so large a scale that it would be appreciated and spread all over the country; for as the sources of education extend, we find more and more need of assisting men who have a disposition for decency and good citizenship. *The mechanic is well paid, and the man who has learned to labor is much more independent than he who is prepared for a profession or a scientific career, or other objects in life that call for higher education:* Clerks commencing at small salaries need good surroundings and economy to give themselves a start. Such are the men for whom the hotels were established."

X

Nordica: What it Costs to Become a Queen of Song

OF the internationally famous singers, none is a greater favorite than Madame Lillian Nordica. She has had honors heaped upon her by every music-loving country. Milan, St. Petersburg, Paris, London and New York, in turn accepted her. Jewel cases filled with bracelets, necklaces, tiaras and diadems, of gold and precious stones, attest the unaffected sincerity of her admirers in all the great music-centers of the world. She enjoys, in addition, the distinction of being one of the first two American women to attain to international fame as a singer in grand opera.

Madame Nordica I met on appointment at the Waldorf-Astoria Hotel, where she kindly detailed for me she encountered at the outset:—" Distinction in the field of art is earned: it is not thrust upon anyone. The material for a great voice may be born in a person—it is, in fact,—but the making of it into a great voice is a work of the most laborious character.

" In some countries the atmosphere is not very favorable to beginners. Almost any of the greater European nations is probably better in this respect than the United States: not much better, however, because nearly all depends upon strength of character, determination, and the will to work. If a girl has these, she will rise as high, in the end, anywhere."

Madame Nordica came of New England stock, being born at Farmington, Maine, and reared in Boston. Her parents, bearing the name Norton, possessed no musical talent. " Their opinion of music," said Madame, " was that it is an airy, inviting art of the devil, used to tempt men's feet to stray from the solemn path of right. They believed music, as a vocation, to be nearly as reprehensible as a stage career, and for the latter they had no tolerance whatever. I must be just, though, and own that they did make an exception in the case of church music, else I should never have received the slightest encouragement in my aspirations. They considered music in churches to be permissible,—even laudable, so when I displayed some ability as a singer, I was allowed to use it in behalf of religion, and I did. I joined the church choir and sang hymns about the house almost constantly.

"But I needed a world of training. I had no conception of what work lay ahead of anyone who contemplates singing perfectly. I had no idea of how high I might go myself. All I knew was that I could sing, and that I would win my way with my voice if I could."

"How did you accomplish it?"

"By devoting all my time, all my thought, and all my energy to that one object. I devoured church music,—all I could get hold of. I practised new and difficult compositions all the time I could spare.

"I became a very good church singer; so much so that when there were church concerts or important religious ceremonies, I was always in demand. Then there began to be a social demand for my ability, and, later, a public demand in the way of concerts.

"At first, I ignored all but church singing. My ambition ran higher than concert singing, and I knew my parents would not consent. I persuaded them to let me have my voice trained. This was not very difficult, because my church singing, as it had improved, became a source of considerable profit; and they saw even greater results for me in the large churches, and in the religious field. So I went to a teacher of vocal culture, Professor John O'Neill, one of the instructors in the New England Conservatory of Music, Boston. He was a fine old teacher, a man with the highest ideals concerning music, and of the sternest and most exacting method. He made me feel, at first, that

THE WORLD WAS MINE, IF I WOULD WORK.

Hard work was his constant cry. There must be no play, no training for lower forms of public entertainment, no anything but study and practice. I must work and perfect myself in private, and then suddenly appear unheralded in the highest class of opera and take the world by storm.

"It was a fine fancy, but it would not have been possible. O'Neill was a fine musician. Under him I studied the physiology of the voice, and practiced singing oratorios. I also took up Italian, familiarizing myself with the language, with all the songs and endless *arias*. In fact, I made myself as perfect in Italian as possible. In *three years* I had been greatly improved. Mr. O'Neill, however, employed methods of making me work which discouraged me. He was a man who would magnify and storm over the slightest error, and make light of or ignore the sincerest achievements. He put his grade of perfection so high that I began to consider it unattainable, and lost heart. Finally, I gave it up and rested awhile, uncertain of everything.

"After I had thought awhile and regained some confidence, I came to New York to see Mme. Maretzek. She was not only a teacher, but also a singer quite famous in her day, and she thoroughly knew the world of music. She considered my voice to be of the right quality for the highest grade of operatic success; and gave me hope that, with a little more training, I could begin my career. She not only did that, but also set me to studying the great operas, 'Lucia' and the others, and introduced me to the American musical celebrities. Together we heard whatever was worth hearing in New York.

"When the renowned Brignola came to New York, she took me to the Everett House, where he was stopping and introduced me. They were good friends, and, after gaining his opinion on the character of my voice, she had him play 'Faust.' That was a wonderful thing for me. To hear the great Brignola! It fired my ambition. As I listened I felt that I could also be great and that people, some day, might listen to me as enraptured as I then was by him.

"IT PUT NEW FIRE INTO ME

and caused me to fairly toil over my studies. I would have given up all my hours if only I had been allowed or requested.

"So it went, until *after several years of study,* Madame Maretzek thought I was getting pretty well along and might venture some important public singing. We talked about different ways of appearing and what I would sing, and so on, until finally Gilmore's band came to Madison Square Garden. He was in the heyday of his success then, and carried important soloists with him. Madame Maretzek decided that she would take me to see him and get his opinion; and so, one day, toward the very last of his Madison Square engagement, we went to see him. Madame Maretzek was on good terms with him also. I remember that she took me in, one morning, when he was rehearsing. I saw a stout, kindly, genial-looking man who was engaged in tapping for attention, calling certain individuals to notice certain points, and generally fluttering around over a dozen odds and ends. Madame Maretzek talked with him a little while and then called his attention to me. He looked toward me.

" 'Thinks she can sing, eh? Yes, yes. Well, all right! Let her come right along.'

" Then he called to me,—'Come right along now. Step right up here on the stage. Yes, yes. Now, what can you sing?'

" I told him I could sing almost anything in oratorio or opera, if he so wished. He said: 'Well, well, have a little from both. Now, what shall it be?'

" I shall never forget his kindly way. He was like a good father, gentle and reassuring, and seemed really pleased to have me there and to hear me. I went up on the platform and told him that I would begin with 'Let the Bright Seraphim,' and he called the orchestra to order and had them accompany me."

" I was slightly nervous at first, but recovered my equanimity and sang up to my full limit of power. When I was through, he remarked, 'Very good! very good!' and 'Now, what else?' I next sang an *aria* from 'Somnambula.' He did not hesitate to express his approval, which was always, 'Very good! very good! Now, what you want to do,' he said, 'is to get some roses in your cheeks, and come along and sing for me.' After that, he continued his conference with Madame Maretzek and then we went away together.

"I WAS TRAVELING ON AIR

when I left, I can assure you. His company was famous. Its engagement had been most successful. Madame Poppenheim was singing with it, and there were other famous names. There were only two more concerts to conclude his New York engagement, but he had told Madame Maretzek that if I chose to come and sing on these occasions, he would be glad to have me. I was more than glad of the opportunity and agreed to go. We arranged with him by letter, and, when the evening came, I sang. My work made a distinct impression on the audience, and pleased Mr. Gilmore wonderfully. After the second night, when all was over, he came to me, and said: 'Now, my dear, of course there is no more concert this summer, but I am going West in the fall. Now, how would you like to go along?'

"I told him that I would like to go very much, if it could be arranged; and, after some negotiation, he agreed to pay the expenses of my mother and myself, and give me one hundred dollars a week besides. I accepted, and when the western tour began, we went along.

"I gained thorough control of my nerves upon that tour, and learned something of audiences, and of what constitutes distinguished 'stage presence.' *I studied all the time,* and, with the broadening influence of travel, gained a great deal. At the end of the tour, my voice was more under my control than ever before, and I was a better singer all around."

"You did not begin with grand opera, after all?"

"No, I did not. It was not a perfect conclusion of my dreams, but it was a great deal. My old instructor, Mr. O'Neill, took it worse than I did. He regarded my ambitions as having all come to naught. I remember that he wrote me a letter in which he thus called me to account:—

" 'After all my training, my advice, that you should come to this! A whole lifetime of ambition and years of the hardest study consumed to fit you to go on the road with a brass band! Poh!'

"I pocketed the sarcasm in the best of humor, because I was sure of my dear old teacher's unwavering faith in me, and knew that he wrote only for my own good. Still, I felt that I was doing wisely in getting before the public, and so decided to wait quietly and see if time would not justify me.

"When the season was over, Mr. Gilmore came to me again. He was the most kindly man I ever knew. His manner was as gentle and his heart as good as could be.

" 'I am going to Europe,' he said. 'I am going to London and Paris and Vienna and Rome, and all the other big cities. There will be a fine chance for you to see all those places and let Europeans hear you. They appreciate good singers. Now, little girl, do you want to come? If you do, you can.' "

"I talked it over with my mother and Madame Maretzek, and decided to go; and so, the next season, we were

IN EUROPE.

"We gave seventy-eight concerts in England and France. We opened the Trocadero at Paris, and mine was the first voice of any kind to sing there. This European tour of the American band was a great and successful venture. American musicians still recall the *furore* which it created, and the prestige which it gained at home. Mr. Gilmore was proud of his leading soloists. In Paris, where the great audiences went wild over my singing, he came to praise me personally in unmeasured terms. 'My dear,' he said, 'you are going to be a great singer. You are going to be crowned in your own country yet. Mark my words: they are going to put diamonds on your brow!' [Madame Nordica had good occasion to recall this, in 1898, many years after, when her enthusiastic New York admirers crowned her with a diamond tiara as a tribute of their admiration and appreciation.]

"It was at the time when Gilmore was at the height of his Paris engagement that his agent ran off with his funds and left the old bandmaster almost stranded. Despite his sincere trouble, he retained his imperturbable good nature, and came out of it successfully. He came to me, one morning, smiling good-naturedly, as usual. After greeting me and inquiring after my health, he said: 'My dear child, you have saved some little money on this tour?' I told him I had.

"'Now, I would like to borrow that little from you.'

"I was very much surprised at the request, for he said nothing whatever of his loss. Still, he had been so uniformly kind and generous, and had won our confidence and regard so wholly, that I could not hesitate. I turned over nearly all I had, and he gathered it up and went away, simply thanking me. Of course, I heard of the defalcation later. It became generally known. Our salaries went right on, howhowever, and in a few months the whole thing had been quite forgotten, when he came to me one morning with money ready in his hand.

"'To pay you what I owe you, my dear,' he said.

"'Oh, yes!' I said; 'so and so much,'—naming the amount.

"'Here it is,' he said; and, handing me a roll of bills, he went away. Of course, I did not count it until a little later; but, when I did, I found just double the amount I had named, and no persuasion would ever induce him to accept a penny of it back."

"When did you part with Gilmore?"

"At the end of that tour. He determined to return to America, and I had decided to spend some of my earnings on further study in Italy. Accordingly, I went to Milan, to the singing teacher San Giovanni. On arriving there, I visited the old teacher and stated my object. I said that I wanted to sing in grand opera.

"'WHY DON'T YOU SING IN GRAND OPERA?'

"He answered; 'let me hear your voice.'

"I sang an *aria* from 'Lucia'; and, when I was through, he said, dryly: 'You want to sing in grand opera?'

"'Yes.'

"'Well, why don't you?'

"'I need training.'

"'Nonsense!' he answered. 'We will attend to that. You need a few months to practice Italian methods,—that is all.'

"So I spent three months with him. After much preparation, I made my *début* as Violetta in Verdi's opera, 'La Traviata,' at the Teatro Grande, in Brescia."

The details of Madame Nordica's Italian appearance are very interesting. Her success was instantaneous. Her fame went up and down the land, and across the water—to her home. She next sang in Gounod's "Faust," at Geneva, and soon afterwards appeared at Navarro, singing Alice in Meyerbeer's "Roberto," the enthusiastic and delighted subscribers presenting her with a handsome set of rubies and pearls. After that, she was engaged to sing at the Russian capital, and accordingly went to St. Petersburg, where, in October, 1881, she made her *dêbut* as La Filma in "Mignon."

There, also her success was great. She was the favorite of the society of the court, and received pleasant attentions from every quarter. Presents were made her, and inducements for her continued presence until two winters had passed. Then she decided to revisit France and Paris.

THIS WAS HER CROWNING TRIUMPH

"I wanted to sing in grand opera at Paris," she said to me. "I wanted to know that I could appear successfully in that grand place. I counted my achievements nothing until I could do that."

"And did you?"

"Yes. In July, 1882, I appeared there."

This was her greatest triumph. In the part of Marguerite, she took the house by storm, and won from the composer the highest encomiums. Subsequently, she appeared with equal success as Ophélie, having been specially prepared for both these rôles by the respective composers, Charles Gounod and Ambroise Thomas.

"You should have been satisfied, after that," I said.

"I was," she answered. "So thoroughly was I satisfied that soon afterwards I gave up my career, and was married. For two years, I remained away from the public; but after that time, my husband having died, I decided to return.

"I made my first appearance at the Burton Theatre in London, and was doing well enough when Colonel Mapleson came to me. He was going to produce grand opera,—in fact he was going to open Covent Garden, which had been closed for a long time, with a big company. He was another interesting character. I found him to be generous and kind-hearted and happy-spirited as anyone could be. When he came to me, it was in the most friendly manner. 'I am going to open Covent Garden,' he said. 'Now, here is your chance to sing there. All the great singers have appeared there. Patti, Gerster, Nilsson, Tietjens; now it's your turn,—come and sing.'

"'How about terms?' I asked.

"'Terms!' he exclaimed; 'terms! Don't let such little details stand in your way. What is money compared to this? Ignore money. Think of the honor, of the memories of the place, of what people think of it.' And then he waved his arms dramatically.

"Yet, we came to terms, not wholly sacrificial on my part, and the season began. Covent Garden had not been open for a long time. It was in the spring of the year, cold and damp. There was a crowded house, though, because fashion accompanied the Prince of Wales there. He came, night after night, and heard the opera through with an overcoat on.

"It was no pleasant task for me, or healthy, either, but the Lord has blessed me with a sound constitution. I sang my parts, as they should be sung—some in bare arms and shoulders, with too little clothing for such a temperature. I nearly froze, but it was Covent Garden and a great London audience, and so I bore up under it.

"Things went on this way very successfully until Sir Augustus Harris took Drury Lane and decided to produce grand opera. He started in opposition to Colonel Mapleson, and so Covent Garden had to be given up. Mr. Harris had more money, more prestige with society, and Colonel Mapleson could not live under the division of patronage. When I saw the situation, I called on the new manager and talked with him concerning the next season. He was very proud and very condescending, and made sure to show his indifference to me. He told me all about the brilliant season he was planning, gave me a list of the great names he intended to charm with, and wound up by saying he would call on me, in case of need, but thought he had all the celebrities he could use, but would let me know.

"Of course, I did not like that; but I knew I could rest awhile, and so was not much disturbed. The time for the opening of the season arrived. The papers were full of accounts of the occasion, and there were plenty of remarks concerning my non-appearance. Then

'Aida' was produced, and I read the criticisms of it with interest.

SHE WAS INDISPENSABLE IN "AIDA"

"The same afternoon a message came for me: 'Would I come?' and 'Would I do so and so?' I would, and did. I sang 'Aida' and then other parts, and gradually all the parts but one, which I had longed to try, but had not yet had the opportunity given to me. I was very successful, and Sir Augustus was very friendly.

"The summer after that season, I visited Ems, where the De Reszkes were. One day they said: 'We are going to Beirut, to hear the music,—don't you want to go along?' I thought it over, and decided that I did. My mother and I packed up and departed. When I got there and saw those splendid performances, I was entranced. It was perfectly beautiful. Everything was arranged after an ideal fashion. I had a great desire to sing there, and boasted to my mother that I would. When I came away, I was fully determined to carry it out."

"Could you speak German?"

"Not at all. I began, though, at once, to

study it; and, when I could talk it sufficiently, I went to Beirut and saw Madame Wagner."

THE KINDNESS OF FRAU WAGNER

"Did you find her the imperious old lady she is said to be?"

"Not at all. She welcomed me most heartily; and, when I told her that I had come to see if I could not sing there, she seemed much pleased. She treated me like a daughter, explained all that she was trying to do, and gave me a world of encouragement. Finally, I arranged to sing and create 'Elsa' after my own idea of it, during the season following the one then approaching.

"Meanwhile I came to New York to fulfill my contract for the season of 1894-1895. While doing that, I made a study of Wagner's, and, indeed, of all German music; and, when the season was over, went back and sang it."

Madame Nordica has found her work very exacting. For it she has needed a good physique; her manner of study sometimes calling for an extraordinary mental strain:—

"I remember once, during my season under Augustus Harris, that he gave a garden party, one Sunday, to which several of his company were invited,—myself included. When the afternoon was well along, he came to me and said: 'Did you ever sing "Valencia" in "The Huguenots?"' I told him I had not.

"'Do you think you could learn the music and sing it by next Saturday night?'

"I felt a little appalled at the question, but ventured to say that I could. I knew that hard work would do it.

"'Then do,' he replied; 'for I must have you sing it.'

"The De Reszkes, Jean and Edouard, were near at the time, and offered to assist me. 'Try it,' they said, and so I agreed. We began rehearsals, almost without study, the very next day, both the De Reszkes prompting me, and by Friday they had me letter-perfect and ready to go on. Since the time seemed so peculiarly short, they feared for me, and, during the performance, stationed themselves, one in either wing, to reassure me. Whenever I approached near to either side of the stage, it was always to hear their repeated 'Be calm!' whispered so loud that the audience could almost hear it. Yet I sang easily, never thinking of failure."

Madame Lillian Nordica

MUSICAL TALENT OF AMERICAN GIRLS

"Let me ask you one thing," I said. "Has America good musical material?"

"As much as any other country, and more, I should think. The higher average of intelligence here should yield a greater percentage of musical intelligence."

"Then there ought to be a number of American women who can do good work of a high order?"

"There ought to be, but it is a question whether there will be. They are not cut out for the work which it requires to develop a good voice. I have noticed that young women seem to *underestimate the cost of distinction.* It means more than most of them are prepared to give; and, when they face the exactions of art, they falter and drop out. Hence we have many middle-class singers, but few really powerful ones."

"What are these exactions you speak of?"

"*Time, money, and loss of friends, of pleasure. To be a great singer means, first, to be a great student. To be a great student means that you have no time for balls and parties, very little for friends, and less for carriage rides and pleasant strolls. All that is really left is a shortened allowance of sleep, of time for meals, and time for exercise.*

THE PRICE OF FAME

"Permanent recognition, which cannot be taken away from you, is acquired only by *a lifetime of most earnest labor.* People are never internationally recognized until they have reached middle life. Many persons gain notoriety young, but that goes as quickly as it comes. *All true success is founded on real accomplishment acquired with difficulty.*

"Many young people have genius; but they need training for valuable service. The world gives very little recognition for a great deal of labor paid in; and, when I earn a thousand dollars for a half hour's singing sometimes, it does not nearly average up for all the years and for the labor much more difficult which I contributed without recompense."

XI

How William Dean Howells Worked to Secure a Foothold

IN answer to my question, what constitutes success in life, Mr. Howells replied that everything is open to the beginner who has sufficient energy, perseverance and brains.

" A young man stands at the parting of two ways," he added, " and can take his path this way or that. It is comparatively easy then, with good judgment. Youth is certainly the greatest advantage which life supplies."

Upon my inquiring about his early life, he replied: " I was born in a little southeastern Ohio village—Martin's Ferry,—which had little of what people deem advantages in schools, railroads, or population. I am not sure, however, that compensation was not had in other things."

As to any special talent for literary composition, Mr. Howells remarked that he came of a reading race, which had always loved literature in a way, and that it was his inclination to read.

Upon this, I ventured to ask: "Would you say that, with a leaning toward a special study, and good health, a fair start, and perseverance, anyone can attain to distinction?"

"That is a probability, only. You may be sure that distinction will not come without those qualities. The only way to succeed, is to have them; although having them will not necessarily guarantee distinction. I can only say that I began with

A LOFTY IDEAL.

"My own youth was not specially marked by advantages. There were none, unless you can call a small bookcase full of books, which my home contained, an advantage. The printing-office was my school from a very early date. My father thoroughly believed in it, and he had his belief as to work, which he illustrated as soon as we were old enough to learn the trade he followed. We could go to school and study, or we could go into the printing-office and work, with perhaps an equal chance of learning; but we could not be idle."

"And you chose the printing-office?"

"Not wholly. As I recall it, I went to and fro between the schoolhouse and the printing-office. When I tired of one, I was promptly given the other.

"As the world goes now, we were poor. My father's income was never above twelve hundred a year, and his family was large; but nobody was rich then. We lived in the simple fashion of that time and place.

"My reading, somehow, went on pretty constantly. No doubt my love for it won me a chance to devote time to it. The length varied with varying times.

"Sometimes I read but little. There were so many years of work—of over-work, indeed, which falls to the lot of many,—that I should be ashamed to speak of it except in accounting for the fact of my little reading. My father had sold his paper in Hamilton, and bought an interest in another at Dayton, and at that time we were all straining our utmost to help pay for it. In that period very few hours were given to literature. My daily tasks began so early, and ended so late, that I had little time, even if I had the spirit for reading. Sometimes I had to sit up until midnight, waiting for telegraphic news, and be up again at dawn to deliver the papers, working afterwards at the case; but that was only for a few years."

ACQUIRING A LITERARY STYLE

"When did you find time to seriously apply yourself to literature?"

"I think I did so before I really had the time. Literary aspirations were stirred in me by the great authors whom I successively discovered, and I was perpetually imitating the writings of these,—modeling some composition of my own after theirs, but never willing to own it."

"Do you attribute your style to the composite influence of these various models?"

"No doubt they had their effect, as a whole, but individually I was freed from the last by each succeeding author, until at length I came to understand that I must be like myself, and no other."

"Had you any conveniences for literary research, beyond the bookcase in your home?"

"If you mean a place to work, I had a narrow, little space, under the stairs. There was a desk pushed back against the wall, which the irregular ceiling sloped down to meet, behind it; and at my left was a window, which gave a good light on the writing leaf of my desk. This was

MY WORKSHOP

for six or seven years,—and it was not at all a bad one. It seemed, for a while, so very simple and easy to come home in the middle of the afternoon, when my task at the printing-office was done, and sit down to my books in my little study, which I did not finally leave until the family were all in bed. My father had a decided bent for literature; and, when I began to show a liking for it, he was eager to direct my choice. This finally changed to merely recommending books, and eventually I was left to my own judgment,—a perplexed and sorrowfully mistaken judgment, at times."

"In what manner did you manage to read the works of all your favorite authors?"

"My hours in the printing-office began at seven and ended at six, with an hour at noon for dinner, which I used for putting down such verses as had come to me in the morning. As soon as supper was over I got out my manuscripts, and sawed, and filed, and hammered away at my blessed poems, which were little less than imitations, until nine, when I went regularly to bed, to rise again at five. Sometimes the foreman gave me an afternoon off on Saturday, which I devoted to literature."

As I questioned further, it was said: "As I recall it, my father had secured one of those legislative clerkships in 1858, which used to fall sometimes to deserving country editors; and together we managed and carried out a scheme for corresponding with some city papers. Going to Columbus, the State Capital, we furnished a daily letter giving an account of the legislative proceedings, which I mainly wrote from the material he helped me to gather. The letters found favor, and my father withdrew from the work wholly. These letters I furnished during two years.

"At the end of the first winter, a Cincinnati paper offered me the city editorship, but one night's round with the reporters at the police station satisfied me that I was not meant for that kind of work. I then returned home for the summer, and spent my time in reading, *and in sending off poems, which regularly came back.* I worked in my father's printing-office; but, as soon as my task was done, went home to my books, and worked away at them until supper. Then a German bookbinder, with whom I was endeavoring to read Heine in the original, met me in my father's editorial room, and with a couple of candles on the table between us, and our Heine and the dictionary before us, we read until we were both tired out."

As to the influence of this constant writing and constant study, Mr. Howells remarked: "It was not without its immediate use. I learned

HOW TO CHOOSE BETWEEN WORDS,

after a study of their fitness; and, though I often employed them decoratively, and with no vital sense of their qualities, still, in mere decoration, they had to be chosen intelligently, and after some thought about their structure and meaning. I could not imitate great writers without imitating their method, which was to the last degree intelligent. They knew what they were doing, and, although I did not always know what I was doing, they made me wish to know, and ashamed of not knowing. The result was beneficial."

Mr. Howells then spoke of his astonishment, when one day he was at work as usual in the printing-office at home, upon being invited to take a place upon a Republican newspaper at Columbus, the Capital; where he was given charge of the news department. This included the literary notices and book reviews, to which, at once, he gave his prime attention.

"When did you begin to contribute to the literature of the day?"

"If you mean, when did I begin to attempt to contribute, I should need to fix an early date, for I early had experience with rejected manuscripts. One of my pieces, upon the familiar theme of Spring, was the first thing I ever had in print. My father offered it to the editor of the paper I worked on in Columbus, where we were then living, and I first knew what he had done, when with mingled shame and pride, I saw it in the journal. In the tumult of my emotions, I promised myself that if I ever got through that experience safely, I would never suffer anything else of mine to be published; but it was not long before I offered the editor a poem, myself."

"When did you publish your first story?"

"My next venture was a story in the Ik Marvel manner, which it was my misfortune to carry into print. I did not really write it, but composed it, rather, in type, at the case. It was not altogether imitated from Ik Marvel, for I drew upon the easier art of Dickens, at times, and helped myself out in places with bold parodies of 'Bleak House.' It was all very well at the beginning, but I had not reckoned with the future sufficiently to start with any clear ending in my mind; and, as I went on, I began to find myself more and more in doubt about it. My material gave out; my incidents failed me; the characters wavered, and threatened to perish in my hands. To crown my misery, there grew up an impatience with the story among its readers; and this found its way to me one day, when I overheard an old farmer, who came in for his paper, say that he 'did not think that story amounted to much.' I did not think so either, but it was deadly to have it put into words, and how I escaped the moral effect of the stroke I do not know. Somehow, I managed to bring the wretched thing to a close, and to live it slowly down.

THE FATE FOLLOWING COLLABORATION

"My next contribution to literature was jointly with John J. Piatt, the poet, who had worked with me as a boy in the printing-office at Columbus. We met in Columbus, where I was then an editor, and we made our first literary venture together in a volume entitled, 'Poems of Two Friends.' *The volume became instantly and lastingly unknown to fame;* the West waited, as it always does, to hear what the East should say. The East said nothing, and two-thirds of the small edition of five hundred copies came back upon the publisher's hands. This did not deter me, however, from contributing to the periodicals, which from time to time, accepted my efforts.

"I remained as an editor, in Columbus, until 1861, when I was appointed

CONSUL AT VENICE.

I really wanted to go to Germany, that I might carry forward my studies in German literature; and I first applied for the Consulate at Munich. The powers at Washington thought it quite the same thing to offer me Rome, but I found that the income of the Roman Consulate would not give me a living, and I was forced to decline it. Then the President's private secretaries, Mr. John Nicolay and Mr. John Hay, who did not know me, except as a young Westerner who had written poems in the 'Atlantic Monthly,' asked me how I would like Venice, promising that the salary would be put up to $1,000 a year. It was really put up to $1,500, and I accepted. I had four years of nearly uninterrupted leisure at Venice."

"Was it easier, when you returned from Venice?"

"Not at all. On my return to America, my literary life took such form that most of my reading was done for review. I wrote at first a good many of the lighter criticisms in 'The Nation;' and then I went to Boston, to become assistant editor of 'The Atlantic Monthly,' where I wrote the literary notices for that periodical for four or five years; then I became editor until 1881. And I have had some sort of close relation with magazines ever since."

"Would you say that all literary success is very difficult to achieve?" I ventured.

"All that is enduring."

"It seems to me ours is an age when fame comes quickly."

"Speaking of quickly made reputations," said Mr. Howells, meditatively, "did you ever hear of Alexander Smith? He was a poet who, in the fifties, was proclaimed immortal by the critics, and ranked with Shakespeare. I myself read him with an ecstasy which, when I look over his work to-day, seems ridiculous. His poem, 'Life-Drama,' was heralded as an epic, and set alongside of 'Paradise Lost.' I cannot tell how we all came out of this craze, but the reading world is very susceptible to such lunacies. He is not the only third-rate poet who has been thus apotheosized, before and since. You might have envied his great success, as I certainly did; but it was not success, after all; and I am sure that real success is always difficult to achieve."

MY LITERARY EXPERIENCE

"Do you believe that success comes to those who have a special bent or taste, which they cultivate by hard work?"

"I can only answer that out of *my literary experience*. For my own part, I believe I have *never got any good from a book, that I did not read merely because I wanted to read it.* I think this may be applied to anything a person does. The book, I know, which you read from a sense of duty, or because for any reason you must, is apt to yield you little. This, I think, is also true of everything, and the endeavor that does one good—and lasting good,—is *the endeavor one makes with pleasure.* Labor done in another spirit will serve in a way, but pleasurable labor brings, on the whole, I think, the greatest reward."

Referring again to his early years, it was remarked: "A definite literary ambition grew up in me; and in the long reveries of the afternoon, when I was distributing my case in the printing-office, I fashioned a future of overpowering magnificence and undying celebrity. I should be ashamed to say what literary triumphs I achieved in those preposterous deliriums. But I realize now that such dreams are nerving, and sustain one in an otherwise barren struggle."

"Were you ever tempted and willing to abandon your object of a literary life for something else?"

"I was, once. My first and only essay aside from literature was in *the realm of law.* It was arranged with a United States Senator that I should study law in his office. I tried it a month, but almost from the first day, I yearned to return to my books. *I had not only to go back to literature, but to the printing-office, and I gladly chose to do it,—a step I never regretted."*

AS TO A HAPPY LIFE,

it was said by Mr. Howells, at the close of our interview:—

"I have come to see life, not as the chase of a forever-impossible personal happiness, but as *a field for endeavor toward the happiness of the whole human family.* There is no other success. I know, indeed, of nothing more subtly satisfying and cheering than a knowledge of the real good will and appreciation of others. Such happiness does not come with money, nor does it flow from a fine physical state. It cannot be bought. But it is the keenest joy, after all; and the toiler's truest and best reward."

XII

JOHN D. ROCKEFELLER

THE richest man in the United States, John Davidson Rockefeller, has consented to break his rule never to talk for publication; and he has told me the story of his early struggles and triumphs, and given utterance to some strikingly interesting observations anent the same. In doing so, he was influenced by the argument that there is something of helpfulness, of inspiration, in the career of every self-made man.

While many such careers have been prolific of vivid contrasts, this one is simply marvelous. Whatever may be said by political economists of the dangers of vast aggregations of wealth in the hands of the few, there can be no question of the extraordinary interest attaching to the life story of a man who was a farm laborer at the age of fifteen, who left school at eighteen, because he felt it to be his duty to care for his mother and brother, and who, at the zenith of his business career, has endowed Chicago University with $7,500,000 out of a fortune estimated at over $300,000,000,—probably the largest single fortune on earth.

The story opens in a fertile valley in Tioga County, New York, near the village of Richford, where John D. Rockefeller was born on his father's farm in July, 1838. The parents of the boy were church-going, conscientious, debt-abhorring folk, who preferred the independence of a few acres to a mortgaged domain. They were Americans to the backbone, intelligent, industrious people, not very poor and certainly not very rich, for at fourteen John hired out to neighboring farmers during the summer months, in order to earn his way and not be dependent upon those he loved. His father was able to attend to the little farm himself, and thus it happened that the youth spent several summers away from home, toiling from sunrise to sunset, and sharing the humble life of the people he served.

HIS EARLY DREAM AND PURPOSE

Did the tired boy, peering from his attic window, ever dream of his future?

He said to a youthful companion of Richford, a farmer's boy like himself: "I would like to own all the land in this valley, as far as I can see. I sometimes dream of wealth and power. Do you think we shall ever be worth one hundred thousand dollars, you and I? I hope to,—some day."

Who can estimate the influence such a life as this must have had upon the future multi-millionaire? I asked Mr. Rockefeller about this, and found him enthusiastic over the advantages which he had received from his rural surroundings, and full of faith in the ability of the country boy to surpass his city cousin.

"To my mind," he said, "there is something unfortunate in being born in a city. Most young men raised in New York and other large centers have not had the struggles which come to us who were reared in the country. It is a noticeable fact that the country men are crowding out the city fellows who have wealthy fathers. They are willing to do more work and go through more for the sake of winning success in the end. Sons of wealthy parents haven't a ghost of a show in competition with the fellows who come from the country with a determination to do something in the world."

The next step in the young man's life was his going to Cleveland, Ohio, in his sixteenth year.

"That was a great change in my life," said he. "Going to Cleveland was my first experience in a great city, and I shall never forget those years. I began work there as an office-boy, and learned a great deal about business methods while filling that position. But what benefited me most in going to Cleveland was the new insight I gained as to what a great place the world really is. I had plenty of ambition then, and saw that, if I was to accomplish much, I would have to work very, very hard, indeed."

SCHOOL DAYS

He found time, during the year 1854, to attend the sessions of the school which is now known as the Central High School. It was a brick edifice, surrounded by grounds which contained a number of hickory trees. It has long since been superseded by a larger and handsomer building, but Andrew J. Freese, the teacher, is still living. It is one of the proudest recollections of this delightful old gentleman's life that John D. Rockefeller went to school with him. I visited him at his residence in Cleveland the other day, and he said:—

"John was one of the best boys I had. He was always polite, but when the other boys threw hickory clubs at him, or attempted any undue familiarities with him, he would stop smiling and sail into them. Young Hanna—Marcus A. Hanna,—who was also a pupil, learned this, to his cost, more than once, and so did young Jones, the present Nevada senator. I have had several very distinguished pupils, you see, and one of my girls is now Mrs. John D. Rockefeller. I had Edward Wolcott, the Colorado senator, later on. Yes, John was about as intelligent and well-behaved a chap as I ever had. Here is one of his essays which you may copy, if you wish."

Mr. Rockefeller, I am quite sure, will pardon me for copying his composition at this late day, for its tone and subject matter reflect credit upon him:—

"Freedom is one of the most desirable of all blessings. Even the smallest bird or insect loves to be free. Take, for instance, a robin that has always been free to fly from tree to tree, and sing its cheerful song from day to day,—catch it, and put it into a cage which is to it nothing less than a prison, and, although it may be there tended with the choicest care, yet it is not content. How eloquently does it plead, though in silence, for liberty. From day to day it sits mournfully upon its perch, meditating, as it were, some way for its escape, and when at last this is effected, how cheerfully does it wing its way out from its gloomy prison-house to sing undisturbed in the branches of the first trees.

" If even the birds of the air love freedom, is it not natural that man, the lord of creation, should? I reply that it is, and that it is a violation of the laws of our country, and the laws of our God, that man should hold his fellowman in bondage. Yet how many thousands there are at the present time, even in our own country, who are bound down by cruel masters to toil beneath the scorching sun of the South. How can America, under such circumstances, call herself free? Is it extending freedom by granting to the South one of the largest divisions of land that she possesses for the purpose of holding slaves? It is a freedom that, if not speedily checked, will end in the ruin of our country."

It was greatly to the regret of the teacher

that John came to him one day to announce his purpose to leave school. Mr. Freese urged him to remain two years longer, in order that he might complete the course, but the young man told him he felt obliged to earn more money than he was getting, because of his desire to provide for his mother and brother. He had received an offer, he said, of a place on the freight docks as a bill clerk, and this job would take him away from his studies.

A RAFT OF HOOP POLES

A short time afterwards, when Mr. Freese visited his former pupil at the freight dock, he found the young man seated on a bale of goods, bill book and pencil in hand. Pointing to a raft of hoop poles in the water, John told his caller that he had purchased them from a Canadian who had brought them across Lake Erie, expecting to sell them. Failing in this, the owner gladly accepted a cash offer from young Rockefeller, who named a price below the usual market rates. The young man explained that he *had saved a little money out of his wages,* and that this was his first speculation. He afterwards told Mr. Freese that he rafted the purchase himself to a flour mill, and disposed of his bargain at a profit of fifty dollars.[1]

THE ODOR OF OIL

It was Mr. Freese, too, who first got the young man interested in oil. They were using sperm oil in those days, at a dollar and a half a gallon. Somebody had found natural petroleum, thick, slimy, and foul-smelling, in the Pennsylvania creeks, and a quantity of it had been received in Cleveland by a next-door neighbor of the schoolmaster. The neighbor thought it could be utilized in some way, but his experiments were as crude as the ill-favored stuff itself. These consisted of boiling, burning, and otherwise testing the oil, and the only result was the incurring of the disfavor of the near-by residents. The young man became interested at once. He, too, experimented with

[1] This hoop pole story is matched by another, related by a friend, of Rockefeller's later warehouse days in Cleveland. He one day bought a lot of beans. He bought them cheap, because they were damaged. Instead of selling them at a slight advance, as most dealers would have done, he spent all his spare time, for weeks, in the attic of his warehouse, sorting over those beans. He took out all the blackened and injured ones, and in the end he got a fancy price for the remainder, because they were of extra quality.

the black slime, draining off the clearer portions and touching matches to it. The flames were sickly, yellow, and malodorous.

"*There must be some way of deodorizing this oil,*" said John, "*and I will find it.* There ought to be a good sale for it for illuminating purposes, if the good oil can be separated from the sediment, and that awful smell gotten rid of."

How well the young man profited by the accidental meeting is a matter of history. But I am digressing.

HIS FIRST LEDGER, AND THE ITEMS IN IT

While in Cleveland, slaving away at his tasks, Mr. Rockefeller was training himself for the more busy days to come. He kept a small ledger in which he entered all his receipts and expenditures, and I had the privilege of examining this interesting little book, and having its contents explained to me. It was nothing more than a small, paper-backed memorandum book.

"When I looked this book up the other day, I thought I had but the cover," said Mr. Rockefeller, "but, on examination, I perceived that I had utilized the cover to write on. In those days I was very economical, just as I am economical now. Economy is a virtue. I hadn't seen my little ledger for a long time, when I found it among some old things. It is more than forty-two years ago since I wrote what it contains. I called it 'Ledger A,' and I wouldn't exchange it now for all the ledgers in New York city and their contents. A glance through it shows me how carefully I kept account of my receipts and disbursements. I only wish more young men could be induced to keep accounts like this nowadays. It would go far toward teaching them the value of money.

"*Every young man should take care of his money. I think it is a man's duty to make all the money he can, keep all he can, and give away all he can.* I have followed this principle religiously all my life, as is evidenced in this book. It tells me just what I did with my money during my first few years in business. Between September, 1855, and January, 1856, I received just fifty dollars. Out of this sum I paid for my washing and my board, and managed to save a little besides. I find, in looking through the book, that I gave a cent to Sunday school every Sunday. It wasn't much, but it was all that I could afford to give to that particular object. *What I could afford to give to the various religious and charitable works, I gave regularly. It is a good habit for a young man to get into.*

"During my second year in Cleveland, I earned twenty-five dollars a month. I was beginning to be a capitalist," said Mr. Rockefeller, "and I suppose I ought to have considered myself a criminal for having so much money. I paid all my own bills at this time, and had some money to give away. I also had the happiness of saving some. I am not sure, but I was more independent then than now. I couldn't buy the most fashionable cut of clothing, but I dressed well enough. I certainly did not buy any clothes I couldn't pay for, as some young men do that I know of. I didn't make any obligations I could not meet, and *my earnest advice is for every young man to live within his means. One of the swiftest 'toboggan slides' I know of, is for a young fellow just starting out into the world to go into debt.*

"During the time between November, 1855, and April, 1856, I paid out just nine dollars and nine cents for clothing. And there is one item that was certainly extravagant as I usually wore mittens in the winter. This item is for fur gloves, two dollars and a half. In this same period *I gave away five dollars and fifty-eight cents. In one month I gave to foreign missions, ten cents, to the mite society, fifty cents, and twelve cents to the Five Points Mission, in New York.* I wasn't living here then, of course, but I suppose I thought the Mission needed money. These little contributions of mine were not large, but they brought me into direct contact with church work, and that has been a benefit to me all my life. It is a mistake for a man to think that he must be rich to help others."

TEN THOUSAND DOLLARS

He earned and saved ten thousand dollars before he was twenty-five years old.

Before he attained his majority, Rockefeller formed a partnership with another young man named Hewett, and began a warehouse and produce business. This was the natural outgrowth of his freight clerkship on the docks. *In five years, he had amassed about ten thousand dollars* besides earning a reputation for business capacity and probity.

John D. Rockefeller

HE REMEMBERED THE OIL

He never forgot those experiments with the crude oil. Discoveries became more and more frequent in the Pennsylvania oil territory. There was a rush of speculators to the new land of fortune. Men owning impoverished farms suddenly found themselves rich. Thousands of excited men bid wildly against each other for newly-shot wells, paying fabulous sums occasionally for dry holes.

KEEPING HIS HEAD

John D. Rockefeller looked the entire field over carefully and calmly. Never for a moment did he lose his head. His Cleveland bankers and business friends had asked him to purchase some wells, if he saw fit, offering to back him up with $75,000 for his own investment [he was worth about $10,000 at the time], and to put in $400,000 more on his report.

The business judgment of this young man at twenty-five was so good, that his neighbors were willing to invest half a million dollars at his bidding.

He returned to Cleveland without investing a dollar. Instead of joining the mad crowd of producers, he sagaciously determined to begin at the other end of the business,—the refining of the product.

THERE WAS MORE MONEY IN A REFINERY

The use of petroleum was dangerous at that time, on account of the highly inflammable gases it contained. Many persons stuck to candles and sperm oil through fear of an explosion if they used the new illuminant. The process of removing these superfluous gases by refining, or distilling, as it was then called, was in its infancy. There were few men who knew anything about it.

Among Rockefeller's acquaintances in Cleveland was one of these men. His name was Samuel Andrews. He had worked in a distillery, and was familiar with the process. He believed that there was a great business to be built up by removing the gases from the crude oil and making it safe for household use. Rockefeller listened to him, and became convinced that he was right. Here was a field as wide as the world, limited only by the production of crude oil. It was a proposition on which he could figure and make sure of the result. It was just the thing Rockefeller had been looking for. He decided to leave the production of oil to others, and to devote his attention to preparing it for market.

Andrews was a brother commission merchant. The two started a refinery, each closing out his former business connection. In two weeks it was running night and day to fill orders. So great was the demand, and so great was the judgment of young Rockefeller,—seeing what no one else had seen.

A second refinery had to be built at once, and in two years their plants were turning out two thousand barrels of refined petroleum per day. Henry M. Flagler, already wealthy, came into the firm, the name of which then became Rockefeller, Flagler and Andrews. More refineries were built, not only at Cleveland, but also at other advantageous points. Competing refineries were bought or rendered ineffective by the cutting of prices.

It is related that Mr. Andrews became one day dissatisfied, and he was asked,—"What will you take for your interest?" Andrews wrote carelessly on a piece of paper,—"One million dollars." Within twenty-four hours he was handed that amount; Mr. Rockefeller saying,—"Cheaper at one million than ten." In building up the refinery business Rockefeller was the head; the others were the hands. He was always the general commanding, the tactician. He made the plans and his associates carried them out. Here was the post for which he had fitted himself, and in which his genius for planning had full sway. In the conduct of the refinery affairs, as in every enterprise in which he has taken part, he exemplified another rule to which he had adhered from his boyhood days. He was the leader in whatever he undertook. In going into any undertaking, John D. Rockefeller has made it his rule to have the chief authority in his own hands or to have nothing to do with the matter.

STANDARD OIL

In 1870, when Mr. Rockefeller was thirty-two years old, the business was merged into the Standard Oil Company, starting with a capital of one million dollars. Other pens have written the later story of that great corporation; how it started pipe lines to carry the oil to the seaboard; how it earned millions in by-products which had formerly run to waste; how it covered the markets of the world in its keen search for trade, distancing all competition, and cheapening its own processes so that its dividends in one year, 1899, amounted to $23,000,000 in excess of the fixed dividend upon the whole capital stock. This is the outcome of thirty years' development. The corporation is now the greatest business combination of modern times, or of any age of the world. Mr. Rockefeller's annual income from his holdings of Standard Oil stock is estimated at about sixteen millions of dollars.

MR. ROCKEFELLER'S PERSONALITY

The brains of all this, the owner of the largest percentage of the stock in the parent corporation, and in most of the lesser ones, is now sixty-two years old. His personality is simple and unaffected, his tastes domestic, and the trend of his thoughts decidedly religious. His Cleveland residential estate is superb, covering a large tract of park-like land,—but even there he has shown his unselfishness by donating a large portion of his land to the city for park purposes. His New York home is not a pretentious place,—solid, but by no means elegant in outward appearance. Between the two homes he divides his time with his wife and children. He is an earnest and hard-working member of the Fifth Avenue Baptist Church, in New York, and does much to promote the good work carried on by that organization. He is particularly interested in the Sunday-school work.

AT THE OFFICE

He arises early in the morning, at his home, and, after a light breakfast, attends to some of his personal affairs there. He is always early on hand at the great Standard Oil building on lower Broadway, New York, and, during the day, he transacts business connected with the management of that vast corporation. There is hardly one of our business men of whom the public at large knows so little. He avoids publicity as most men would the plague. The result is that he is the only one of our very wealthy men who maintains the reputation of being different from the ordinary run of mortals. To most newspaper readers, he is a man of mystery, a sort of financial wizard who sits in his office and heaps up wealth after the fashion of Aladdin and other fairy-tale heroes.

All this is wide of the mark. It would be hard to find a more commonplace, matter-of-fact man than John D. Rockefeller. His tall form, with the suggestion of a stoop in it, his pale, thoughtful face and reserved manner, suggest the scholar or professional man rather than an industrial Hercules or a Napoleon of finance. He speaks in a slow, deliberate manner, weighing each word. There is nothing impulsive or bombastic about him. But his conversation impresses one as consisting of about one hundred per cent. of cold, compact, boiled-down common sense.

Here is to be noted one characteristic of the great oil magnate which has helped to make him what he is. The popular idea of a multi-millionaire is a man who has taken big risks, and has come out luckily. He is a living refutation of this conception. He is careful and cautious by nature, and he has made these traits habitual for a lifetime; he conducts all his affairs on the strictest business principles.

FORESIGHT

The qualities which have made him so successful are largely those which go to the making of any successful business man,—industry, thrift, perseverance, and foresight. Three of these qualities would have made him a rich man; the last has distinguished him as the richest man. One of his business associates said of him, the other day:—

"I believe the secret of his success, so far as there is any secret, lies in power of foresight, which often seems to his associates to be wonderful. It comes simply from his habit of looking at every side of a question, of weighing the favorable and unfavorable features of a situation, and of sifting out the inevitable result through his unfailing good judgment."

This is his own personal statement, put into other words, so it may be accepted as true. The encouraging part of it is that, while such foresight as Rockefeller displays may be ascribed partly to natural endowment, both he and his friend say that it is more largely a matter of habit, made effective by continual practice.

HYGIENE

At noon he takes a very simple lunch at his club, or at some downtown restaurant. The lunch usually consists of a bowl of bread and milk. He remains at the office until late in the afternoon, and before dinner he takes some exercise. *In winter, he skates when possible.* And at other seasons of the year he nearly always drives in the park or on the avenues. Mr. Rockefeller has great faith in fresh air as a tonic.

AT HOME

The evenings are nearly always spent at home, for neither Mr. Rockefeller nor any of the children are fond of " society," as the word is understood in New York. The children seem to have inherited many of their father's sensible ideas, and John D. Rockefeller, Jr., has apparently escaped the fate of most rich men's sons. He has a deep sense of responsibility as the heir-apparent to so much wealth; and, since his graduation from college, he has devoted himself to a business career, starting at the bottom and working upward, step by step. It is now generally known that he has been very successful in his business ventures, and he bids fair to become a worthy successor to his father. He is now actively engaged in important philanthropic enterprises in New York. Miss Bessie became the wife of a poor clergyman of the Baptist Church in Cleveland; while Miss Alta is married to a prominent young business man in Chicago.

PHILANTHROPY

Mr. Rockefeller has during many years turned over to his children a great many letters from needy people, asking them to exercise their own judgment in distributing charities.

While he has himself given away millions for education and charity, he would have given more were it not for his dread of seeming ostentatious. But he never gives indiscriminately, nor out of hand. When a charity appeals to him, he investigates it thoroughly, just as he would a business scheme. If he decides that its object is worthy, he gives liberally; otherwise, not a cent can be got out of him.

It may be imagined that such a man is busy to the full limit of his working capacity. This is true. He is too busy for any of the pastimes and pleasures in which most wealthy men seek diversion. He is thoroughly devoted to his home and family, and spends as much as possible of his time with them. He is a man who views life seriously, but in his quiet way he can get as much enjoyment out of a good story or a meeting with an old friend as can any other man.

John D. Rockefeller

PERSEVERANCE

When I asked Mr. Rockefeller what he considers has most helped him in obtaining success in business, he answered: "It was early training, and the fact that I was willing to persevere. I do not think there is any other quality so essential to success of any kind as the quality of perseverance. It overcomes almost everything, even nature."

It is to be said of his business enterprises, looking at them in a large way, that he has given to the world good honest oil, of standard quality; that his employees are always well paid; that he has given away more money in benevolence than any other business man in America. And everything about the man indicates that he is likely to "persevere" in the course he has so long pursued, turning his vast wealth into institutes for public service.

A GENIUS FOR MONEY MAKING

"There are men born with a genius for money-making," says Mathews. "They have the instinct of accumulation. The talent and the inclination to convert dollars into doubloons by bargains or shrewd investments are in them just as strongly marked and as uncontrollable as were the ability and the inclination of Shakespeare to produce Hamlet and Othello, of Raphael to paint his cartoons, of Beethoven to compose his symphonies, or Morse to invent an electric telegraph. As it would have been a gross dereliction of duty, a shameful perversion of gifts, had these latter disregarded the instincts of their genius and engaged in the scramble for wealth, so would a Rothschild, an Astor, and a Peabody have sinned had they done violence to their natures, and thrown their energies into channels where they would have proved dwarfs and not giants."

The opportunity which came to young Rockefeller does not occur many times in many ages: and in a generous interpretation of his opportunity he has already invested a great deal of his earnings in permanently useful philanthropies.

XIII

The Author of the Battle Hymn of the Republic--Her Views of Education for Young Women

A POET, author, lecturer, wit and conversationalist, Mrs. Julia Ward Howe unites with the attributes of a tender, womanly nature—which has made her the idol of her husband and children—the sterner virtues of a reformer; the unflinching courage which dares to stand with a small minority in the cause of right; the indomitable perseverance and force of character which persist in the demand for justice in face of the determined opposition of narrow prejudice and old-time conservatism.

Although more Bostonian than the Bostonians themselves, Mrs. Howe first saw the light in New York, and has spent much of her later life at Newport. Born in 1819, in a stately mansion near the Bowling Green, then the most fashionable quarter of New York, she was the fourth child of Samuel Ward and Julia Cutler Ward, people of unusual culture, refinement, and high ideals. Mr. Ward was a man of spotless honor and business integrity; and, although not wealthy as compared with the millionaires of to-day, his fortune was ample enough to surround his wife and children with all the luxuries and refinements that the most fastidious nature could crave. Mrs. Ward possessed a rare combination of personal charms and mental gifts, which endeared her to all who had the privilege of knowing her. All too soon, the death angel came and bore away the lovely young wife and mother, then in her twenty-eighth year.

Rousing himself, with a great effort, from the grief into which the death of his wife had plunged him, Mr. Ward devoted himself to the training, and education of his children. Far in advance of his age in the matter of higher education for women he selected as the tutor of his daughters the learned Doctor Joseph Green Cogswell, with instruction to teach them the full curriculum of Harvard college.

Mrs. Julia Ward Howe

"LITTLE MISS WARD"

The scholarly and refined atmosphere of her father's home, which was the resort of the most distinguished men of letters of the day, was an admirable school for the development of the literary and philosophic mind of the "little Miss Ward," as Mr. Ward's eldest daughter had been called from childhood.

Learned even beyond advanced college graduates of to-day, an accomplished linguist, a musical amateur of great promise, the young and beautiful Miss Julia Ward, of Bond street, soon became a leader of the cultured and fashionable circle in which she moved. In the series, "Authors at Home," by M. C. Sherwood, we get a glimpse of her, about that time, in a whimsical entry from the diary of a Miss Hamilton, written at the time of the return of Doctor Howe, from Greece, whither he had gone to fight the Turks:—

"I walked down Broadway with all the fashion and met the pretty blue stocking, Miss Julia Ward, with her admirer, Doctor Howe, just home from Europe. She had on a blue satin cloak and a white muslin dress. I looked to see if she had on blue stockings, but I think not. I suspect that her stockings were pink, and she wore low slippers, as grandmamma does. They say she dreams in Italian and quotes French verses. She sang very prettily at a party last evening. I noticed how white her hands were. Still, though attractive, the muse is not handsome."

SHE MARRIED A REFORMER

Soon after the loss of her father, in 1839, Miss Ward paid the first of a series of visits to Boston, where she met, among other distinguished people who became life-long friends, Sarah Margaret Fuller, Horace Mann, Charles Sumner, and Ralph Waldo Emerson. In 1843 she was married to the director of the institute for the blind, in South Boston, the physician and reformer, Doctor Samuel G. Howe, of whom Sydney Smith spoke—referring to the remarkable results attained in his education of Laura Bridgman,—as "a modern Pygmalion who has put life into a statue." Immediately after their marriage, Doctor and Mrs. Howe sailed for Europe, making London their first stopping place. There they met many famous men and women, among them Charles Dickens,

Thomas Carlyle, Sydney Smith, Thomas Moore, the Duchess of Sutherland, John Forster, Samuel Rogers, Richard Monckton Milnes, and many others. After an extensive continental tour, including the Netherlands, Switzerland, Germany, France, and Italy, Doctor and Mrs. Howe returned home and took up their residence in South Boston.

One of her friends has said: "Mrs. Howe wrote leading articles from her cradle;" and it is true that at seventeen, at least, she was an anonymous but valued contributor to the *New York Magazine*, then a prominent periodical. In 1854, her first volume of poems was published. She named it "Passion Flowers," and the Boston world of letters hailed her as a new poet. Though published anonymously, the volume at once revealed its author; and Mrs. Howe was welcomed into the poetic fraternity by such shining lights as Emerson, Whittier, Longfellow, Bryant, and Holmes. The poem by which the author will be forever enshrined in her country's memory is, *par excellence*, "The Battle Hymn of the Republic," which, like Kipling's "Recessional," sang itself at once into the heart of the nation. As any sketch of Mrs. Howe would be incomplete without the story of the birth of this great song of America, it is here given in brief.

STORY OF THE "BATTLE HYMN OF THE REPUBLIC"

It was in the first year of our Civil War that Mrs. Howe, in company with her husband and friends, visited Washington. During their stay in that city, the party went to see a review of troops, which, however, was interrupted by a movement of the enemy, and had to be put off for the day. The carriage in which Mrs. Howe was seated with her friends was surrounded by armed men; and, as they rode along, she began to sing, to the great delight of the soldiers, "John Brown." "Good for you!" shouted the boys in blue, who, with a will, took up the refrain. Mrs. Howe then began conversing with her friends on the momentous events of the hour, and expressed the strong desire she felt to write some words which might be sung to this stirring tune, adding that she feared she would never be able to do so. "She went to sleep," says her daughter, Maude Howe Eliot, "full of thoughts of battle, and awoke before dawn the next morning to find the desired verses immediately present to her mind. She sprang from her bed, and in the dim gray light found a pen, and paper, whereon she wrote, scarcely seeing them, the lines of the poem. Returning to her couch, she was soon asleep, but not until she had said to herself, 'I like this better than anything I have ever written before.'"

"EIGHTY YEARS YOUNG"

Of Mrs. Howe it may very fittingly be said that she is eighty years young. Her blue eye retains its brightness, and her dignified carriage betokens none of the feebleness of age. Above all, her mind seems to hold, in a marvelous degree, its youthful vigor and elasticity; a fact that especially impressed me as the author of "The Battle Hymn of the Republic" expressed her views on the desirability of a college training for girls.

"The girls who go to college," said Mrs. Howe, "are very much in request, I should say for everything,—certainly for teaching. Then, naturally, if they wish to follow literature, they have a very great advantage over those who have not had the benefit of a college course, having a liberal education to begin with."

"Which is the greater advantage to a girl, to have talent or great perseverance?"

"In order to accomplish anything really worth doing, I think great perseverance is of the first importance. On the other hand, one cannot do a great deal without talent, while special talent without perseverance never amounts to much. I once heard Mr. Emerson say, 'Genius without character is mere friskiness;' and we all know of highly gifted people, who, because lacking the essential quality of perseverance, accomplish very little in the world."

"Do you think the college girl will exercise a greater influence on modern progress and the civilization of the future than her untrained sister?"

"Oh, very much greater," was the quick, emphatic reply. "In the first place, I think that college-bred girls are quite as likely to marry as others, and when a college girl marries, then the whole family is lifted to a higher plane, the natural result of the well-trained, cultivated mind. Mothers of old, you know, were very ignorant. Indeed, it is sad to think what few advantages they had. Of course, some of them had opportunities to study alone, but this solitary study could not accomplish for them what the colleges, with their corps of specialists and trained professors, are doing for the young women of to-day."

THE IDEAL COLLEGE

Speaking of the advantages and disadvantages of coeducational institutions, Mrs. Howe said:—

"While there are many advantages in coeducation, there are also some dangers. The great advantage consists in the mingling of both sorts of mind, the masculine and the feminine. This gives a completeness that cannot otherwise be obtained. I have observed that when committees are made up of both men and women, we get a roundness and completeness that are lacking when the membership is composed of either sex alone; and so in college recitations, where the boys present their side and the girls theirs, we get better results. This, of course, is natural. Fortunately, so far, scandals have been very rare, if found at all, in coeducation at colleges. Many people, however, would not care to trust their children, nor would we send every girl, to such colleges; and, for this reason, I am glad that we have women's colleges. I think, however, that, if the students are at all earnest, and have high ideals set before them, the coeducational is the ideal college; for the course in these colleges is like a great intellectual race, which arouses and stimulates all the nobler faculties."

"What influence do you think environment has on one's career,—on success in life?"

"What do you mean by environment?"

"Well, I mean especially the sort of people with whom one is associated; their order of mind?"

"I think it has a very important effect. If we are kept perpetually under lowering influences—lowering both morally and æsthetically,—the tendency will inevitably be to drag us down. I say æsthetically, because I think in that sense good taste is a part of good morals. You can, of course, have good taste without good morals; but with morality there is a certain feeling or measure of reserve and nicety which does not accompany good taste without good morals. You know St. Paul says: 'Evil communications corrupt good manners.' That is as true to-day as it ever was. We can't always be with our equals or our superiors, however; we must take people as we find them.

But we should try to be with people who stand for high things, morally and intellectually. Then, when we have to be among people of a lower grade, we can help them, because I think human nature, on the whole, desires to be elevated rather than lowered."

"Do you think it is necessary to success in life to have a special aim?"

"I think it is a great thing to have a special aim or talent, and it is better to make one thing the leading interest in life than to run after half-a-dozen."

XIV

A TALK WITH EDISON

DRAMATIC INCIDENTS IN HIS EARLY LIFE

TO discover the opinion of Thomas A. Edison concerning what makes and constitutes success in life is an easy matter—if one can first discover Mr. Edison. I camped three weeks in the vicinity of Orange, N. J., awaiting the opportunity to come upon the great inventor and voice my questions. It seemed a rather hopeless and discouraging affair until he was really before me; but, truth to say, he is one of the most accessible of men, and only reluctantly allows himself to be hedged in by pressure of endless affairs.

" Mr. Edison is always glad to see any visitor," said a gentleman who is continually with him, " except when he is hot on the trail of something he has been working for, and then it is as much as a man's head is worth to come in on him."

He certainly was not hot on the trail of anything on the morning when, for the tenth time,

Thomas A. Edison

I rang at the gate in the fence which surrounds the laboratory on Valley Road, Orange. A young man appeared, who conducted me up the walk to the Edison laboratory office.

THE LIBRARY

is a place not to be passed through without thought, for, with a further store of volumes in his home, it contains one of the most costly and well-equipped scientific libraries in the world; the collection of writings on patent laws and patents, for instance, is absolutely exhaustive. It gives, at a glance, an idea of the breadth of thought and sympathy of this man who grew up with scarcely a common school education.

On the second floor, in one of the offices of the machine-shop, I was asked to wait, while a grimy youth disappeared with my card, which he said he would "slip under the door of Mr. Edison's office."

"Curious," I thought; "what a lord this man must be if they dare not even knock at his door!"

Thinking of this and gazing out the window, I waited until a working man, who had entered softly, came up beside me. He looked with a sort of "Well, what is it?" in his eyes, and quickly it began to come to me that the man in the sooty, oil-stained clothes was Edison himself. The working garb seemed rather incongruous, but there was no mistaking the broad forehead, with its shock of blackish hair streaked with gray. The gray eyes, too, were revelations in the way of alert comprehensiveness.

"Oh!" was all I could get out at the time.

"Want to see me?" he said, smiling in the most youthful and genial way.

"Why,—yes, certainly, to be sure," I stammered.

He looked at me blankly.

"You'll have to talk louder," said an assistant who worked in another portion of the room; "he don't hear well."

This fact was new to me, but I raised my voice with celerity, and piped thereafter in an exceedingly shrill key. After the usual humdrum opening remarks, in which he acknowledged his age as fifty-two years, and that he was born in Erie county, O., of Dutch parentage, the family having emigrated to America in 1730, the particulars began to grow more interesting.

His great-grandfather, I learned, was a banker of high standing in New York; and, when Thomas was but a child of seven years, the family fortune suffered reverses so serious as to make it necessary that he should become a wage-earner at an unusually early age, and that the family should move from his birthplace to Michigan.

"Did you enjoy mathematics as a boy?" I asked.

"Not much," he replied. "I tried to read Newton's 'Principia,' at the age of eleven. That disgusted me with pure mathematics, and I don't wonder now. I should not have been allowed to take up such serious work."

"You were anxious to learn?"

"Yes, indeed, *I attempted to read through the entire Free Library at Detroit,* but other things interfered before I had done."

A CHEMICAL NEWSBOY

"Were you a book-worm and dreamer?" I questioned.

"Not at all," he answered, using a short, jerky method, as though he were unconsciously checking himself up. "I became a newsboy, and liked the work. Made my first *coup* as a newsboy in 1869."

"What was it?" I ventured.

"I bought up on 'futures' a thousand copies of the *Detroit Free Press* containing important war news,—gained a little time on my rivals, and sold the entire batch like hot cakes. The price reached twenty-five cents a paper before the end of the route," and he laughed. "I ran the *Grand Trunk Herald,* too, at that time—a little paper I issued from the train."

"When did you begin to be interested in invention?" I questioned.

"Well," he said, "I began to dabble in chemistry at that time. I fitted up a small laboratory on the train."

In reference to this, Mr. Edison subsequently admitted that, during the progress of some occult experiments in this workshop, certain complications ensued in which a jolted and broken bottle of sulphuric acid attracted the attention of the conductor. He, who had been long suffering in the matter of unearthly odors, promptly ejected the young devotee and all his works. This incident would have been only amusing but for its relation to, and explanation of, his deafness. A box on the ear, administered by the irate conductor, caused the lasting deafness.

TELEGRAPHY

"What was your first work in a practical line?" I went on.

"A telegraph line between my home and another boy's, I made with the help of an old river cable, some stove-pipe wire, and glass-bottle insulators. I had my laboratory in the cellar and studied telegraphy outside."

"What was the first really important thing you did?"

"I saved a boy's life."

"How?"

"The boy was playing on the track near the depot. I saw he was in danger and caught him, getting out of the way just in time. His father was station-master, and taught me telegraphy in return."

Dramatic situations appear at every turn of this man's life. He seems to have been continually arriving on the scene at critical moments, and always with the good sense to take things in his own hands. The chance of learning telegraphy only gave him a chance to show how apt a pupil he was, and the railroad company soon gave him regular employment. At seventeen, he had become one of the most expert operators on the road.

"Did you make much use of your inventive talent at this time?" I questioned.

"Yes," he answered. "I invented an automatic attachment for my telegraph instrument which would send in the signal to show I was awake at my post, when I was comfortably snoring in a corner. I didn't do much of that, though," he went on; " for some such boyish trick sent me in disgrace over the line into Canada."

"Were you there long?"

"Only a winter. If it's incident you want, I can tell you one of that time. The place where I was and Sarnier, the American town, were cut off from telegraphic and other means of communication by the storms, until I got at a locomotive whistle and tooted a telegraphic message. I had to do it again and again, but eventually they understood over the water and answered in the same way."

According to his own and various recorded accounts, Edison was successively in charge of important wires in Memphis, Cincinnati, New Orleans, and Louisville. He lived in the free-

and-easy atmosphere of the tramp operators—a boon companion with them, yet absolutely refusing to join in the dissipations to which they were addicted. So highly esteemed was he for his honesty, that it was the custom of his colleagues, when a spree was on hand, to make him the custodian of those funds which they felt obliged to save. On a more than usually hilarious occasion, one of them returned rather the worse for wear, and knocked the treasurer down on his refusal to deliver the trust money; the other depositors, we may be glad to note, gave the ungentlemanly tippler a sound thrashing.

HIS USE OF MONEY

"Were you good at saving your own money?" I asked.

"No," he said, smiling. "I never was much for saving money, as money. I devoted every cent, regardless of future needs, to scientific books and materials for experiments."

"You believe that an excellent way to succeed?"

"Well, it helped me greatly to future success."

INVENTIONS

"What was your next invention?" I inquired.

"An automatic telegraph recorder—a machine which enabled me to record dispatches at leisure, and send them off as fast as needed."

"How did you come to hit upon that?"

"Well, at the time, I was in such straits that I had to walk from Memphis to Louisville. At the Louisville station they offered me a place. I had perfected a style of handwriting which would allow me to take legibly from the wire, long hand, forty-seven and even fifty-four words a minute, but I was only a moderately rapid sender. I had to do something to help me on that side, and so I thought out that little device."

Later I discovered an article by one of his biographers, in which a paragraph referring to this Louisville period, says:—

"True to his dominant instincts, he was not long in gathering around him a laboratory, printing office, and machine shop. He took press reports during his whole stay, including on one occasion, the Presidential message, by Andrew Johnson, and this at one sitting, from 3.30 P. M. to 4.30 A. M.

"He then paragraphed the matter he had received over the wires, so that printers had exactly three lines each, thus enabling them to set up a column in two or three minutes' time. For this, he was allowed all the exchanges he desired, and the Louisville press gave him a dinner."

"How did you manage to attract public attention to your ability?" I questioned.

"I didn't manage," said the Wizard. "Some things I did created comment. A device that I invented in 1868, which utilized one sub-marine cable for two circuits, caused considerable talk, and the Franklin telegraph office of Boston gave me a position."

It is related of this, Mr. Edison's first trip East, that he came with no ready money and in a rather dilapidated condition. His colleagues were tempted by his "hayseed" appearance to "salt" him, as professional slang terms the process of giving a receiver matter faster than he can record it. For this purpose, the new man was assigned to a wire manipulated by a New York operator famous for his speed. But there was no fun at all. Notwithstanding the fact that the New Yorker was in the game and was doing his most speedy clip, Edison wrote out the long message accurately, and, when he realized the situation, was soon firing taunts over the wire at the sender's slowness.

"Had you patented many things up to the time of your coming East?" I queried.

"Nothing," said the inventor, ruminatively. "I received my first patent in 1869."

"For what?"

"A machine for recording votes, and designed to be used in the State Legislature."

"I didn't know such machines were in use," I ventured.

"They ar'n't," he answered, with a merry twinkle. "The better it worked, the more impossible it was; the sacred right of the minority, you know,—couldn't filibuster if they used it,—didn't use it."

"Oh!"

"Yes, it was an ingenious thing. Votes were clearly pointed and shown on a roll of paper, by a small machine attached to the desk of each member. I was made to learn that such an innovation was out of the question, but it taught me something."

"And that was?"

"To be sure of the practical need of, and demand for, a machine, before expending time and energy on it."

"Is that one of your maxims of success?"

"It is. It is a good rule to give people something they want, and they will pay money to get it."

HIS ARRIVAL AT THE METROPOLIS

In this same year, Edison removed from Boston to New York, friendless and in debt on account of the expenses of his experiment. For several weeks he wandered about the town with actual hunger staring him in the face. It was a time of great financial excitement, and with that strange quality of Fortunism, which seems to be his chief characteristic, he entered the establishment of the Law Gold Reporting Company just as their entire plant had shut down on account of an accident in the machinery that could not be located. The heads of the firm were anxious and excited to the last degree, and a crowd of the Wall street fraternity waited about for the news which came not. The shabby stranger put his finger on the difficulty at once, and was given lucrative employment. In the rush of the metropolis, a man finds his true level without delay especially when his talents are of so practical and brilliant a nature as were this young telegrapher's. It would be an absurdity to imagine an Edison hidden in New York. Within a short time, he was presented with a check for $40,000, as his share of a single invention—an improved stock printer. From this time, a national reputation was assured him. He was, too, now engaged upon the duplex and quadruplex systems—systems for sending two and four messages at the same time over a single wire,—which were to inaugurate almost a new era in telegraphy.

MENTAL CONCENTRATION

Recalling the incident of the Law Gold Reporting Company, I inquired: "Do you believe want urges a man to greater efforts, and so to greater success?"

"It certainly makes him keep a sharp lookout. I think it does push a man along."

"Do you believe that invention is a gift, or an acquired ability?"

"I think it's born in a man."

"And don't you believe that familiarity with certain mechanical conditions and defects naturally suggests improvements to any one?"

"No. Some people may be perfectly familiar with a machine all their days, knowing it inefficient, and never see a way to improve it."

"What do you think is the first requisite for success in your field, or any other?"

"*The ability to apply your physical and mental energies to one problem incessantly without growing weary.*"

TWENTY HOURS A DAY

"Do you have regular hours, Mr. Edison?" I asked.

"Oh," he said, "I do not work hard now. I come to the laboratory about eight o'clock every day and go home to tea at six, and then I study or work on some problem until eleven, which is my hour for bed."

"Fourteen of fifteen hours a day can scarcely be called loafing," I suggested.

"Well," he replied, "for fifteen years I have worked on an average of twenty hours a day."

When he was forty-seven years old, he estimated his true age at eighty-two, since working only eight hours a day would have taken till that time.

Mr. Edison has sometimes worked sixty consecutive hours upon one problem. Then after a long sleep, he was perfectly refreshed and ready for another.

A RUN FOR BREAKFAST

Mr. Dickson, a neighbor and familiar, gives an anecdote told by Edison which well illustrates his untiring energy and phenomenal endurance. In describing his Boston experience, Edison said he bought Faraday's works on electricity, commenced to read them at three o'clock in the morning and continued until his room-mate arose, when they started on their long walk to get breakfast. That object was entirely subordinated in Edison's mind to Faraday, and he suddenly remarked to his friend: "'Adams, I have got so much to do, and life is so short, that I have got to hustle,' and with that I started off on a dead run for my breakfast."

"I've known Edison since he was a boy of fourteen," said another friend; "and of my own knowledge I can say he never spent an idle day in his life. Often, when he should have been asleep, I have known him to sit up half the night reading. He did not take to novels or wild Western adventures, but read works on mechanics, chemistry, and electricity; and he mastered them too. But in addition to his reading, which he could only indulge in at odd hours, he carefully cultivated his wonderful powers of observation, till at length, when he was not actually asleep, it may be said he was learning all the time."

NOT BY ACCIDENT AND NOT FOR FUN

"Are your discoveries often brilliant intuitions? Do they come to you while you are lying awake nights?" I asked him.

"I never did anything worth doing by accident," he replied, "nor did any of my inventions come indirectly through accident, except the phonograph.[1] No, when I have fully decided that a result is worth getting, I go about it, and make trial after trial, until it comes.

[1] "I was singing to the mouthpiece of a telephone," said Edison, "when the vibrations of my voice caused a fine steel point to pierce one of my fingers held just behind it. That set me to thinking. If I could record the motions of the point and send it over the same surface afterward, I saw no reason why the thing would not talk. I determined to make a machine that would work accurately, and gave my assistants the necessary instructions, telling them what I had discovered. That's the whole story. The phonograph is the result of the pricking of a finger."

"I have always kept," continued Mr. Edison, "strictly within the lines of commercially useful inventions. I have never had any time to put on electrical wonders, valuable only as novelties to catch the popular fancy."

"I LIKE IT—I HATE IT"

"What makes you work?" I asked with real curiosity. "What impels you to this constant, tireless struggle? You have shown that you care comparatively nothing for the money it makes you, and you have no particular enthusiasm for the attending fame. What is it?"

"I like it," he answered, after a moment of puzzled expression. "I don't know any other reason. Anything I have begun is always on my mind, and I am not easy while away from it, until it is finished; and then I hate it."

"Hate it?" I said.

"Yes," he affirmed, "when it is all done and is a success, I can't bear the sight of it. I haven't used a telephone in ten years, and I would go out of my way any day to miss an incandescent light."[1]

---

[1] "After I have completed an invention," remarked Edison, upon another occasion, "I seem to lose interest

Thomas A. Edison

DOING ONE THING EIGHTEEN HOURS IS THE SECRET

"You lay down rather severe rules for one who wishes to succeed in life," I ventured, "working eighteen hours a day."

"Not at all," he said. "You do something all day long, don't you? Every one does. If you get up at seven o'clock and go to bed at eleven, you have put in sixteen good hours, and it is certain with most men, that they have been doing something all the time. They have been either walking, or reading, or writing, or thinking. The only trouble is that they do it about a great many things and I do it about one. If they took the time in question and applied it in one direction, to one object, they would succeed. Success is sure to follow such

---

in it. One might think that the money value of an invention constitutes its reward to the man who loves his work. But, speaking for myself, I can honestly say this is not so. Life was never more full of joy to me, than when, a poor boy, I began to think out improvements in telegraphy, and to experiment with the cheapest and crudest appliances. But now that I have all the appliances I need, and am my own master, I continue to find my greatest pleasure, and so my reward, in the work that precedes what the world calls success."

application. The trouble lies in the fact that people do not have an object—one thing to which they stick, letting all else go. Success is the product of the severest kind of mental and physical application."

POSSIBILITIES IN THE ELECTRICAL FIELD

"You believe, of course," I suggested, "that much remains to be discovered in the realm of electricity?"

"It is the field of fields," he answered. "We can't talk of that, but it holds the secrets which will reorganize the life of the world."

"You have discovered much about it," I said, smiling.

"Yes," he said, "and yet very little in comparison with the possibilities that appear."

ONLY SIX HUNDRED INVENTIONS

"How many inventions have you patented?"

"Only six hundred," he answered, "but I have made application for some three hundred more."

"And do you expect to retire soon, after all this?"

"I hope not," he said, almost pathetically.

" I hope I will be able to work right on to the close. I shouldn't care to loaf."

HIS COURTSHIP AND HIS HOME

The idea of the great electrician's marrying was first suggested by an intimate friend, who told him that his large house and numerous servants ought to have a mistress. Although a very shy man, he seemed pleased with the proposition, and timidly inquired whom he should marry. The friend, annoyed at his apparent want of sentiment, somewhat testily replied,—" Anyone." But Edison was not without sentiment when the time came. One day, as he stood behind the chair of a Miss Stillwell, a telegraph operator in his employ, he was not a little surprised when she suddenly turned round and said:

" Mr. Edison, I can always tell when you are behind me or near me."

It was now Miss Stillwell's turn to be surprised, for, with characteristic bluntness and ardor, Edison fronted the young lady, and, looking her full in the face, said:

" I've been thinking considerably about you of late, and, if you are willing to marry me, I would like to marry you."

The young lady said she would consider the matter, and talk it over with her mother. The result was that they were married a month later, and the union proved a very happy one.

It was in fact no more an accident than other experiments in the Edison laboratory—his bride having been long the subject of the Wizzard's observation—her mental capacity, her temper and temperament, her aptitude for home-making being duly tested and noted.

General Lew Wallace in his study.

(*See page 241.*)

XV

A FASCINATING STORY

BY GENERAL LEW WALLACE

IN his study, a curiously-shaped building lighted from the top, and combining in equal portions the Byzantine, Romanesque and Doric styles of architecture, the gray-haired author of "Ben-Hur," surrounded by his pictures, books, and military trophies, is spending, in serene and comfortable retirement, the evening of his life. As I sat beside him, the other day, and listened to the recital of his earlier struggles and later achievements, I could not help contrasting his dignified bearing, careful expression, and gentle demeanor, with another occasion in his life, when, as a vigorous, black-haired young military officer, in the spring of 1861, he appeared, with flashing eye and uplifted sword, at the head of his regiment, the gallant and historic Eleventh Indiana Volunteers.

General Wallace never repels a visitor, and his greeting is cordial and ingenuous.

"If I could say anything to stimulate or encourage the young men of to-day," he said, "I would gladly do so, but I fear that the story of my early days would be of very little interest or value to others. So far as school education is concerned, it may be truthfully said that I had but little, if any; and if, in spite of that deficiency, I ever arrived at proficiency, I reached it, I presume, as Topsy attained her stature,—'just growed into it.'"

A BOYHOOD OF WASTED OPPORTUNITIES

"Were you denied early school advantages?" I asked.

"Not in the least. On the contrary, I had most abundant opportunity in that respect.

"My father was a lawyer, enjoying a lucrative practice in Brookville, Indiana,—a small town which bears the distinction of having given to the world more prominent men than any other place in the Hoosier State. Not long after my birth, he was elected lieutenant-governor, and, finally, governor of the state. He, himself, was an educated man, having been graduated from the United States Military Academy at West Point, and having served as instructor in mathematics there. He was not only an educated man, but a man of advanced ideas generally, as shown by the fact that *he failed of a re-election to congress in* 1840, *because, as a member of the committee on commerce, he gave the casting vote in favor of an appropriation to develop Morse's magnetic telegraph.*

"Of course, he believed in the value, and tried to impress upon me the necessity of a thorough school training. But, in the face of all the solicitude and encouragement which an indulgent father could waste on an unappreciative son, I remained vexatiously indifferent. I presume I was like some man in history,—it was Lincoln, I believe,—who said that his father taught him to work, but he never quite succeeded in teaching him to love it.

"My father sent me to school, and regularly paid tuition,—for in those days there were no free schools; but, much to my discredit, he failed to secure anything like regular attendance at recitations, or even a decent attempt to master my lessons at any time. In fact, much of the time that should have been given to school was spent in fishing, hunting, and roaming through the woods."

HIS BOYHOOD LOVE FOR HISTORY AND LITERATURE

"But were you thus indifferent to all forms of education?"

"No, my case was not quite so hopeless as that. I did not desert the schools entirely, but my attendance was so provokingly irregular and my indifference so supreme, I wonder now that I was tolerated at all. But I had one mainstay; I loved to read. I was a most inordinate reader. In some lines of literature, especially history and some kinds of fiction, my appetite was insatiate, and many a day, while my companions were clustered together in the old red brick schoolhouse, struggling with their problems in fractions or percentage, I was carefully hidden in the woods near by, lying upon my elbows, munching an apple, and reveling in the beauties of Plutarch, Byron or Goldsmith."

"Did you not attend college, or the higher grade of schools?"

"Yes, for a brief period. My brother was a student in Wabash College,—here in Crawfordsville,—and hither I also was sent; but within six weeks I had tired of the routine, was satiated with discipline, and made my exit from the institution.

"I shall never forget what my father did when I returned home. He called me into his office, and, reaching into one of the pigeon-holes above his desk, withdrew therefrom a package of papers neatly folded and tied with the conventional red tape. He was a very systematic man, due, perhaps, to his West Point training, and these papers proved to be the receipts for my tuition, which he had carefully preserved. He called off the items, and asked me to add them together. The total, I confess, staggered me.

A FATHER'S FRUITFUL WARNING

"'That sum, my son,' he said, with a tone of regret in his voice, 'represents what I have expended in these many years past to provide you with a good education. How successful I have been, you know better than anyone else.'

"'After mature reflection, I have come to the conclusion that I have done for you in that direction all that can reasonably be expected of any parent; and I have, therefore, called you in to tell you that you have now reached an age when you must take up the lines yourself. If you have failed to profit by the advantages with which I have tried so hard to surround you, the responsibility must be yours. I shall not upbraid you for your neglect, but rather pity you for the indifference which you have shown to the golden opportunities you have, through my indulgence, been enabled to enjoy.' "

A MANHOOD OF SPLENDID EFFORT

"What effect did his admonition have on you? Did it awaken or arouse you?"

"It aroused me, most assuredly. It set me to thinking as nothing before had done. The next day, I set out with a determination to accomplish something for myself. My father's injunction rang in my ears. New responsibilities rested on my shoulders, as I was, for the first time in my life, my own master. I felt that I must get work on my own account.

"After much effort, I finally obtained employment from the man with whom I had passed so many afternoons strolling up and down the little streams in the neighborhood, trying to fish. He was the county clerk, and he hired me to copy what was known as the complete record of one of the courts. I worked for months in a dingy, half-lighted room, receiving for my pay something like ten cents per hundred words. The tediousness and

THE RECULARITY OF THE WORK WAS A SPLENDID DRILL FOR ME,

and taught me the virtue of persistence as one of the avenues of success. It was at this time I began to realize *the deficiency in my education,* especially as I had an ambition to become a lawyer. Being deficient in both mathematics and grammar, *I was forced to study evenings.* Of course, the latter was a very exacting study, after a full day's hard work; but I was made to realize that *the time I had spent with such lavish prodigality could not be recovered,* and that I must extract every possible good out of the golden moments then flying by all too fast."

SELF-EDUCATION BY READING AND LITERARY COMPOSITION

"Had you a distinct literary ambition at that time?"

"Well, I had always had a sort of literary

bent or inclination. I read all the literature of the day, besides the standard authors, and finally began to devote my odd moments to a book of my own,—a tale based on the days of the crusades. When completed, it covered about three hundred and fifty pages, and bore the rather high-sounding title, 'The Man-at-Arms.' I read a good portion of it before a literary society to which I belonged; the members applauded it, and I was frequently urged to have it published.

"The Mexican War soon followed, however, and I took the manuscript with me when I enlisted. But before the close of my service it was lost, and my production, therefore, never reached the public eye."

"But did not the approval which the book received from the few persons who read it encourage you to continue writing?"

"Fully fifty years have elapsed since then, and it is, therefore, rather difficult, at this late day, to recall just how such things affected me. I suppose I was encouraged thereby, for, in due course of time, another book which turned out to be my first book to reach the public,—began to shape itself in my mind. The composition of this work was not, as the theatrical people would say, a continuous performance, for there were many and singular interruptions; and it would be safe to say that months, and, in one case, years, intervened between certain chapters. A few years after the war, I finished the composition, strung the chapters into a continuous narrative, leveled up the uneven places, and started East with the manuscript. A letter from Whitelaw Reid, then editor of the New York *Tribune*, introduced me to the head of one of the leading publishing houses in Boston. There I was kindly received, and delivered my manuscript, which was referred to a professional reader, to determine its literary, and also, I presume, its commercial value.

"It would be neither a new nor an interesting story to acquaint the public with the degree of anxious suspense that pervaded my mind when I withdrew to await the reader's judgment. Every other writer has, I assume, at one time or another, undergone much the same experience. It was not long until I learned from the publisher that the reader reported in favor of my production. Publication soon followed, and for the first time, in a literary sense, I found myself before the public, and my book before the critics."

THE ORIGIN OF "BEN-HUR"

"How long after this did 'Ben-Hur' appear, and what led you to write it?"

"I began 'Ben-Hur' about 1876, and it was published in 1880. The purpose, at first, was a short serial for one of the magazines, descriptive of the visit of the wise men to Jerusalem as mentioned in the first two verses of the second chapter of Matthew. It will be recognized in 'Book First' of the work as now published. For certain reasons, however, the serial idea was abandoned, and the narrative, instead of ending with the birth of the Saviour, expanded into a more pretentious novel and only ended with the death scene on Calvary. The last ten chapters were written in the old adobe palace at Santa Fé, New Mexico, where I was serving as governor.

"It is difficult to answer the question, 'what led me to write the book;' or why I chose a piece of fiction which used Christ as its leading character. In explanation, it is proper to state that I had reached an age in life when men usually begin to study themselves with reference to their fellowmen, and reflect on the good they may have done in the world. *Up to that time, never having read the Bible,* I knew nothing about sacred history; and, in matters of a religious nature, although I was not in every respect an infidel, I was persistently and notoriously indifferent. *I did not know, and therefore, did not care.* I resolved to begin the study of the good book in earnest.

INFLUENCE OF THE STORY OF THE CHRIST UPON THE AUTHOR

"I was in quest of knowledge, but I had no faith to sustain, no creed to bolster up. The result was that the whole field of religious and biblical history opened up before me; and, my vision not being clouded by previously formed opinions, I was enabled to survey it without the aid of lenses. I believe I was thorough and persistent. I know I was conscientious in my search for the truth. I weighed, I analyzed, I counted and compared. The evolution from conjecture into knowledge, through opinion and belief, was gradual but irresistible; and at length I stood firmly and defiantly on the solid rock.

"Upward of seven hundred thousand copies of 'Ben-Hur' have been published, and it has been translated into all languages from French to Arabic. But, whether it has ever influenced the mind of a single reader or not, I am sure its conception and preparation—if it has done nothing more—have convinced its author of the divinity of the lowly Nazarene who walked and talked with God."

XVI

Carnegie as a Metal Worker

"THERE is no doubt," said Mr. Carnegie, in reply to a question from me, "that it is becoming harder and harder, as business gravitates more and more to immense concerns, for a young man without capital to get a start for himself, and in the large cities it is especially so, where large capital is essential. Still it can be honestly said that there is no other country in the world, where able and energetic young men and women can so readily rise as in this. A president of a business college informed me, recently, that he has never been able to supply the demand for capable, first-class [Mark the adjective.] bookkeepers, and his college has over nine hundred students. In America, young men of ability rise with most astonishing rapidity."

"As quickly as when you were a boy?"

"Much more so. When I was a boy, there were but very few important positions that a boy could aspire to. Every position had to be made. Now a boy doesn't need to make the place,—all he has to do is to fit himself to take it."

EARLY WORK AND WAGES

"Where did you begin life?"'

"In Dunfermline, Scotland, during my earliest years. The service of my life has all been in this country."

"In Pittsburg?"

"Largely so. My father settled in Allegheny City, when I was only ten years old, and I began to earn my way in Pittsburg."

"Do you mind telling me what your first service was?"

"Not at all. I was a bobbin boy in a cotton factory, then an engine-man or boy in the same place, and later still I was a messenger boy for a telegraph company."

"At small wages, I suppose?"

"One dollar and twenty cents a week was what I received as a bobbin boy, and I considered it pretty good, at that. When I was thirteen, I had learned to run a steam engine, and for that I received a dollar and eighty cents a week."

"You had no early schooling, then?"

"None except such as I gave myself."

COLONEL ANDERSON'S BOOKS

"There were no fine libraries then, but in Allegheny City, where I lived, there was a certain Colonel Anderson, who was well to do and of a philanthropic turn. He announced, about the time I first began to work, that he would be in his library at home, every Saturday, ready to lend books to working boys and men. He had only about four hundred volumes, but I doubt if ever so few books were put to better use. Only he who has longed, as I did for Saturday to come, that the spring of knowledge might be opened anew to him, can understand what Colonel Anderson did for me and others of the boys of Allegheny. Quite a number of them have risen to eminence, and I think their rise can be easily traced to this splendid opportunity." [1]

[1] It was Colonel Anderson's kindness that led Carnegie to bestow his wealth so generously for founding libraries, as he is now doing every year.

HIS FIRST GLIMPSE OF PARADISE

"How long did you remain an engine-boy?"

"Not very long," Mr. Carnegie replied; "perhaps a year."

"And then?"

"I entered a telegraph office as a messenger boy."

Although Mr. Carnegie did not dwell much on this period, he once described it at a dinner given in honor of the American Consul at Dunfermline, Scotland, when he said:—

"I awake from a dream that has carried me away back to the days of my boyhood, the day when the little white-haired Scottish laddie, dressed in a blue jacket, walked with his father into the telegraph office in Pittsburg to undergo examination as an applicant for a position as messenger boy.

"Well I remember when my uncle spoke to my parents about it, and my father objected, because I was then getting one dollar and eighty cents per week for running the small engine in a cellar in Allegheny City, but my uncle said a messenger's wages would be two dollars and fifty cents . . . If you want an idea as to heaven on earth, imagine what it is to be taken from a dark cellar, where I fired the boiler from morning until night, and dropped into an office, where light shone from all sides, with books, papers, and pencils in profusion around me, and oh, the tick of those mysterious brass instruments on the desk, annihilating space and conveying intelligence to the world. This was my first glimpse of paradise, and I walked on air."

"How did you manage to rise from this position?"

"I learned how to operate a telegraph instrument, and then waited an opportunity to show that I was fit to be an operator. Eventually my chance came."

The truth is that James D. Reid, the superintendent of the office, and himself a Scotchman, favored the ambitious lad. In his "History of the Telegraph," he says of him:—

"I liked the boy's looks, and it was easy to see that, though he was little, he was full of spirit. He had not been with me a month when he asked me to teach him to telegraph. He spent all his spare time in practice, sending and receiving by sound and not by tape, as was the custom in those days. Pretty soon he could do as well as I could at the key."

INTRODUCED TO A BROOM

"As you look back upon it," I said to Mr. Carnegie, "do you consider that so lowly a beginning is better than one a little less trying?"

"For young men starting upon their life work, it is much the best to begin as I did, at the beginning, and occupy the most subordinate positions. Many of the present-day leading men of Pittsburg, had serious responsibility thrust upon them at the very threshold of their careers. They were introduced to the broom, and spent the first hours of their business life sweeping out the office. I notice we have janitors and janitresses now in offices, and our young men, unfortunately, miss that salutary branch of early education. It does not hurt the newest comer to sweep out the office."

"Did you?"

"Many's the time. And who do you suppose were my fellow sweepers? David McBargo, afterwards superintendent of the Allegheny Valley Railroad; Robert Pitcairn, afterwards superintendent of the Pennsylvania Railroad; and Mr. Mooreland, subsequently City Attorney of Pittsburg. We all took turns, two each morning doing the sweeping; and now I remember Davie was so proud of his clean shirt bosom that he used to spread over it an old silk handkerchief which he kept for the purpose, and we other boys thought he was putting on airs. So he was. None of us had a silk handkerchief."

"After you had learned to telegraph, did you consider that you had reached high enough?"

"Just at that time my father died, and the burden of the support of the family fell upon me. I earned as an operator twenty-five dollars a month, and a little additional money by copying telegraphic messages for the newspapers, and managed to keep the family independent."

AN EXPERT TELEGRAPHER

More light on this period of Mr. Carnegie's career is given by the "*Electric Age,*" which says:—"As a telegraph operator he was abreast of older and experienced men; and, although receiving messages by sound was, at that time, forbidden by authority as being unsafe, young Carnegie quickly acquired the art, and he can still stand behind the ticker and understand its language. As an operator, he delighted in full employment and the prompt discharge of business, and a big day's work was his chief pleasure."

"How long did you remain with the telegraph company?"

"Until I was given a place by the Pennsylvania Railroad Company."

"As an operator?"

"At first,—until I showed how the telegraph could minister to railroad safety and success; then I was made secretary to Thomas A. Scott, the superintendent; and not long afterwards, when Colonel Scott became vice-president, I was made superintendent of the western division."

Colonel Scott's attention was drawn to Carnegie by the operator's devising a plan for running trains by telegraph, so making the most of a single track. Up to this time no one had ever dreamed of running trains in opposite directions, towards each other, directing them by telegraph, one train being sidetracked while the other passed. The boy studied out a train-despatching system which was afterwards used on every single-track railroad in the country. Nobody had ever thought of this before, and the officials were so pleased with the ingenious lad, that they placed him in charge of a division office, and before he was twenty made him superintendent of the western division of the road.

WHAT EMPLOYERS THINK OF YOUNG MEN

Concerning this period of his life, I asked Mr. Carnegie if his promotion was not a matter of chance, and whether he did not, at the time, feel it to be so. His answer was emphatic.

"Never. Young men give all kinds of reasons why, in their cases, failure is attributable to exceptional circumstances, which rendered success impossible. Some never had a chance, according to their own story. This is simply nonsense. No young man ever lived who had not a chance, and a splendid chance, too, if he was ever employed at all. He is assayed in the mind of his immediate superior, from the day he begins work, and, after a time, if he has merit, he is assayed in the council chambers of the firm. His ability, honesty, habits, associations, temper, disposition,—all these are weighed and analyzed. The young man who never had a chance is the same young man who has been canvassed over and over again by his superiors, and found destitute of necessary qualifications, or is deemed unworthy of closer relations with the firm, owing to some objectionable act, habit or association, of which he thought his employers ignorant."

"It sounds true."

"It is."

THE RIGHT MEN IN DEMAND

"Another class of young men attributes failure to rise to employers having near relatives or favorites whom they advance unfairly. They also insist that their employers dislike brighter intelligences than their own, and are disposed to discourage aspiring genius, and delighted in keeping young men down. There is nothing in this. On the contrary, there is no one suffering more for lack of the right man in the right place as the average employer, nor anyone more anxious to find him."

"Was this your theory on the subject when you began working for the railroad company?"

"I had no theory then, although I have formulated one since. It lies mainly in this: Instead of the question, 'What must I do for my employer?' substitute, 'What can I do?' Faithful and conscientious discharge of duties assigned you is all very well, but the verdict in such cases generally is that you perform your present duties so well, that you would better continue performing them. Now, this will not do. It will not do for the coming partners. There must be something beyond this. We make clerks, bookkeepers, treasurers, bank tellers of this class, and there they remain to the end of the chapter. *The rising man must do something exceptional, and beyond the range of his special department. He must attract attention."*

HOW TO ATTRACT ATTENTION

"How can he do that?"

"Well, if he is a shipping clerk, he may do so by discovering in an invoice an error with which he has nothing to do and which has escaped the attention of the proper party. If a weighing clerk, he may save for the firm in questioning the adjustment of the scales, and having them corrected, even if this be the province of the master mechanic. If a messenger boy, he can lay the seed of promotion by going beyond the letter of his instructions in order to secure the desired reply. There is no service so low and simple, neither any so high, in which the young man of ability and willing disposition cannot readily and almost daily prove himself capable of greater trust and usefulness, and, what is equally important, show his invincible determination to rise."

"In what manner did you reach out to establish your present great fortune?" I asked.

"By saving my money. I put a little money aside, and it served me later as a matter of credit. Also, I invested in a sleeping-car industry, which paid me well."

SLEEPING-CAR INVENTION

Although I tried earnestly to get the great iron-king to talk of this, he said little, because the matter has been fully dealt with by him in his "Triumphant Democracy." From his own story there, it appears that one day at this time, when Mr. Carnegie still had his fortune to make, he was on a train examining the line from a rear window of a car, when a tall, spare man, accosted him and asked him to look at an invention he had made. He drew from a green bag a small model of a sleeping-berth for railway cars, and proceeded to point out its advantages. It was Mr. T. T. Woodruff, the inventor of the sleeping-car. As Mr. Carnegie tells the story:—

"He had not spoken a moment before, like a flash, the whole range of the discovery burst upon me. 'Yes,' I said, 'that is something which this continent must have,'

"Upon my return, I laid it before Mr. Scott, declaring that it was one of the inventions of the age. He remarked: 'You are enthusiastic, young man, but you may ask the inventor to come and let me see it.' I did so, and arrangements were made to build two trial cars, and run them on the Pennsylvania Railroad. I was offered an interest in the venture, which I gladly accepted.

"The notice came that my share of the first payment was $217.50. How well I remember the exact sum. But two hundred and seventeen dollars and a half were as far beyond my means as if it had been millions. I was earning fifty dollars per month, however, and had prospects, or at least I always felt that I had. I decided to call on the local banker and boldly ask him to advance the sum upon my interest in the affair. He put his hand on my shoulder and said: 'Why, of course, Andie; you are all right. Go ahead. Here is the money.'

"It is a proud day for a man when he pays his last note, but not to be named in comparison with the day in which he makes his first one, and gets a banker to take it. I have tried both, and I know. The cars furnished the subsequent payments by their earnings. I paid my first note from my savings, so much per month, and thus I got my foot upon fortune's ladder. It was easy to climb after that."

THE MARK OF A MILLIONAIRE

"I would like some expression from you," I said to Mr. Carnegie, "in reference to the importance of laying aside money from one's earnings, as a young man."

"You can have it. There is one sure mark of the coming partner, the future millionaire; his revenues always exceed his expenditures. He begins to save early, almost as soon as he begins to earn. I should say to young men, no matter how little it may be possible to save, save that little. Invest it securely, not necessarily in bonds, but in anything which you have good reason to believe will be profitable. Some rare chance will soon present itself for investment. The little you have saved will prove the basis for an amount of credit utterly surprising to you. Capitalists trust the saving man. For every hundred dollars you can produce as the result of hard-won savings, Midas, in search of a partner, will lend or credit a thousand; for every thousand, fifty thousand. *It is not capital that your seniors require, it is the man who has proved that he has the business habits which create capital. So it is the first hundred dollars that tell.*"

AN OIL-FARM

"What," I asked Mr. Carnegie, "was the next enterprise with which you identified yourself?"

"In company with several others, I purchased the now famous Storey farm, on Oil Creek, Pennsylvania, where a well had been bored and natural oil struck the year before. This proved a very profitable investment."

In "Triumphant Democracy," Mr. Carnegie has expatiated most fully on this venture, which is so important. "When I first visited this famous well," he says, "the oil was running into the creek, where a few flat-bottomed scows lay filled with it, ready to be floated down the Alleghany River, on an agreed-upon day each week, when the creek was flooded by means of a temporary dam. This was the beginning of the natural-oil business. We purchased the farm for $40,000, and so small was our faith in the ability of the earth to yield for any considerable time the hundred barrels per day, which the property was then producing, that we decided to make a pond capable of holding one hundred thousand barrels of oil, which, we estimated, would be worth, when the supply ceased, $1,000,000.

"Unfortunately for us, the pond leaked fearfully; evaporation also caused much loss, but we continued to run oil in to make the losses good day after day, until several hundred thousand barrels had gone in this fashion. Our experience with the farm is worth reciting: its value rose to $5,000,000; that is—the shares of the company sold in the market upon this basis; and one year it paid cash dividends of $1,000,000—upon an investment of $40,000."

IRON BRIDGES

"Were you satisfied to rest with these enterprises in your hands?" I asked.

"No. Railway bridges were then built almost exclusively of wood, but the Pennsylvania Railroad had begun to experiment with cast-iron. It struck me that the bridge of the future must be of iron; and I organized, in Pittsburg, a company for the construction of iron bridges. That was the Keystone Bridge Works. We built the first iron bridge across the Ohio."

His entrance of the realm of steel was much too long for Mr. Carnegie to discuss, although he was not unwilling to give information relating to the subject. It appears that he realized the immensity of the steel manufacturing business at once. The Union Iron Mills soon followed as one of the enterprises, and, later, the famous Edgar Thompson Steel Rail Mill. The last was the outcome of a visit to England, in 1868, when Carnegie noticed that English railways were discarding iron for steel rails. The Bessemer process had been then perfected, and was making its way in all the iron-producing countries. Carnegie, recognizing that it was destined to revolutionize the iron business, introduced it into his mills and made steel rails with which he was enabled to compete with English manufacturers.

HOMESTEAD STEEL WORKS

His next enterprise was the purchase of the Homestead Steel Works,—his great rival in Pittsburg. In 1888, he had built or acquired seven distinct iron and steel works, all of which are now included in the Carnegie Steel Company, Limited. All the plants of this great firm are within a radius of five miles of Pittsburg. Probably in no other part of the world can be found such an aggregation of splendidly equipped steel works as those controlled by this association. It now comprises the Homestead Steel Works, the Edgar Thompson Steel Works and Furnaces, the Duquesne Steel Works and Furnaces, all within two miles of one another; the Lucy Furnaces, the Keystone Bridge Works, the Upper Union Rolling Mills, and the Lower Union Rolling Mills.

In all branches, including the great coke works, mines, etc., there are employed twenty-five thousand men. The monthly pay roll exceeds one million, one hundred and twenty-five thousand dollars, or nearly fifty thousand dollars for each working day. Including the Frick Coke Company, the united capital of the Carnegie Steel Company exceeds sixty million dollars.

A STRENGTHENING POLICY

"You believe in taking active measures," I said, "to make men successful."

Partial view of the Homestead Steel Works.

"I believe in anything which will help men to help themselves. To induce them to save, every workman in our company is allowed to deposit part of his earnings, not exceeding two thousand dollars, with the firm, on which the high interest rate of six per cent. is allowed. The firm also lends to any of its workmen to buy a lot, or to build a house, taking its pay by installments."

"Has this contributed to the success of your company?"

"I think so. The policy of giving a personal interest to the men who render exceptional service is strengthening. With us there are many such, and every year several more are added as partners. It is the policy of the concern to interest every superintendent in the works, every head of a department, every exceptional young man. Promotion follows exceptional service, and there is no favoritism."

PHILANTHROPY

"All you have said so far, merely gives the idea of getting money, without any suggestion as to the proper use of great wealth. Will you say something on that score?"

"My views are rather well known, I think. What a man owns is already subordinate, in America, to what he knows; but in the final aristocracy, the question will not be either of these, but what has he done for his fellows? Where has he shown generosity and self-abnegation? Where has he been a father to the fatherless? And the cause of the poor, where has he searched that out?"

That Mr. Carnegie has lived up in the past, and is still living up to this radical declaration of independence from the practice of men who have amassed fortunes around him, will be best shown by a brief enumeration of some of his almost unexampled philanthropies. His largest gift has been to the city of Pittsburg, the scene of his early trials and later triumphs. There he has built, at a cost of more than a million dollars, a magnificent library, museum, concert hall and picture gallery, all under one roof, andendowed it with a fund of another million, the interest of which (fifty thousand dollars per annum) is being devoted to the purchase of the best works of American art. Other libraries, to be connected with this largest as a center, are now being constructed, which will make the city of Pittsburg and its environs a beneficiary of his generosity to the extent of five million dollars.

While thus endowing the city where his fortune was made, he has not forgotten other places endeared to him by association or by interest. To the Allegheny Free Library he has given \$375,000; to the Braddock Free Library, \$250,000; to the Johnstown Free Library, \$50,000; and to the Fairfield (Iowa) Library, \$40,000. To the Cooper Institute, New York, he has given \$300,000. To his native land he has been scarcely less generous. To the Edinburgh Free Library he has given \$250,000, and to his native town of Dunfermline, \$90,000. Other Scottish towns to the number of ten have received helpful donations of amounts not quite so large. He has given \$50,000 to aid poor young men and women to gain a musical education at the Royal College of Music in London.

"THE MISFORTUNE OF BEING RICH MEN'S SONS"

"I should like to cause you to say some other important things for young men to learn and benefit by."

"Our young partners in the Carnegie company have all won their spurs by *showing that we did not know half as well what was wanted as they did.* Some of them have acted upon occasions with me as if they owned the firm and I was but some airy New Yorker, presuming to *advise upon what I knew very little about.* Well, they are not now interfered with. *They were the true bosses,—the very men we were looking for.*"

"Is this all for the poor boy?"

"Every word. Those who have the misfortune to be rich men's sons are heavily weighted in the race. A basketful of bonds is the heaviest basket a young man ever had to carry. He generally gets to staggering under it. The vast majority of rich men's sons are unable to resist the temptations to which wealth subjects them, and they sink to unworthy lives. It is not from this class that the poor beginner has rivalry to fear. The partner's sons will never trouble you much, but look out that some boys poorer, much poorer, than yourselves, whose parents cannot afford to give them any schooling, do not challenge you at the post and pass you at the grand stand. Look out for the boy who has to plunge into work direct from the common school, and begins by sweeping out the office. He is the probable dark horse that will take all the money and win all the applause." [1]

---

[1] Mr. Carnegie's recent retirement from business, and the sale of his vast properties to the Morgan Syndicate, marks a new era in his remarkable career; and it gives him the more leisure to consider carefully every dollar he bestows in the series of magnificent charities that he has inaugurated.

XVII

Herreshoff, the Yacht Builder

I

THE VOYAGE OF LIFE

**Total eclipse; no sun, no moon;
Darkness amid the blaze of noon!—MILTON**

AMID the ranks of the blind, we often find men and women of culture and general ability, but we do not look for world-renowned specialists. No one is surprised at a display of enterprise in a " booming " western town, where everybody is " hustling; " but in a place which has once ranked as the third seaport in America, but has seen its maritime glory decline, a man who can establish a marine industry on a higher plane than was ever before known, and attract to his work such world-wide attention as to restore the vanished fame of his town, is no ordinary person. Moreover, if such a man has laid his plans and done his work in the disheartening eclipse of total blindness, he must possess qualities of the highest order.

The office of the Herreshoff Manufacturing Company, at Bristol, Rhode Island, is in a building that formerly belonged to the Burnside Rifle Company. It is substantial, but unpretentious, and is entered by a short stairway on one side. The furniture throughout is also plain, but has been selected with excellent taste, and is suggestive of the most effective adaptation of means to ends in every detail. On the mantel and on the walls are numerous pictures, most of them of vessels, but very few relating directly to any of the great races for the "America's" cup. The first picture to arrest one's attention, indeed, is an excellent portrait of the late General Ambrose E. Burnside, who lived in Bristol, and was an intimate friend of John B. Herreshoff.

Previous inquiry had elicited the information that the members of the firm are very busy with various large orders, in addition to the rush of work on Cup Defenders; so it was a very agreeable surprise when I was invited into the tasteful private office, where the blind president sat, having just concluded a short conversation with an attorney.

"LET THE WORK SHOW"

"Well, sir," said he, rising and grasping my hand cordially, "what do you wish?"

"I realize how very busy you must be, Mr. Herreshoff," I replied, and will try to be as brief as possible; but I venture to ask a few minutes of your time, to obtain suggestions and advice from you to young people."

"But why select me, in particular, as an adviser?"

This was "a poser," at first, especially when he added, noting my hesitation:—

"We are frequently requested to give interviews in regard to our manufacturing business; but, since as it is the settled policy of our house to do our work just as well as we possibly can and then leave it to speak for itself, we have felt obliged to decline all these requests. It would be repugnant to our sense of propriety to talk in public about our special industry. 'Let the work show!' seems to us a good motto."

THE VOYAGE OF LIFE

"True," said I. "But the readers of my books may not care to read of cutters or 'skimming dishes,' center-boards or fin keels, or copper coils *versus* steel tubes for boilers. They leave the choice in such matters to you, realizing that you have always proved equal to the situation. What I want now is advice in regard to the race of life,—the voyage in which each youth must be his own captain, but in which the words of others who have successfully sailed the sea before will help to avoid rocks and shoals, and to profit by favoring currents and trade winds. You have been handicapped in an unusual degree, sailing in total darkness and beset by many other difficulties, but have, nevertheless, made a very prosperous voyage. In overcoming such serious obstacles, you must have learned much of the true philosophy of both success and failure, and I think you will be willing to help the young with suggestions drawn from your experience."

"I always want to help young people, or old people, either, for that matter, if anything I can say will do so. But what can I say?"

A MOTHER'S MIGHTY INFLUENCE

"What do you call the prime requisite of success?"

"I shall have to answer that by a somewhat humorous but very shrewd suggestion of another,—select a good mother. Especially for boys, I consider an intelligent, affectionate but considerate mother an almost indispensable requisite to the highest success. If you would improve the rising generation to the utmost, appeal first to the mothers."

"In what way?"

"*Above all things else, show them that reasonable self-denial is a thousandfold better for a boy than to have his every wish gratified. Teach them to encourage industry, economy, concentration of attention and purpose, and indomitable persistence.*"

"But most mothers try to do this, don't they?"

"Yes, in a measure; but many of them, perhaps most of them, do not emphasize the matter half enough. A mother may wish to teach all these lessons to her son, but she thinks too much of him, or believes she does, to have him suffer any deprivation, and so indulges him in things which are luxuries for him, under the circumstances, rather than necessaries. Many a boy, born with ordinary intellect, would follow the example of an industrious father, were it not that his mother wishes him to appear as well as any boy in the neighborhood. So, without exactly meaning it, she gets to making a show of her boy, and brings him up with a habit of idling away valuable time, to keep up appearances. The prudent mother, however, sees the folly of this course, and teaches her son to excel in study and work, rather than in vain display. The difference in mothers makes all the difference in the world to children, who like brooks, can be turned very easily in their course of life."

SELF HELP

"What ranks next in importance?"

"Boys and girls themselves, especially as they grow older, and have a chance to understand what life means, should not only help their parents as a matter of duty, but should learn to help themselves, for their own good. I would not have them forego recreation, a reasonable amount every day, but let them learn the reality and earnestness of existence, and resolve to do the whole work and the very best work of thorough, reliable young men and women."

WHAT CAREER

"What would you advise as to choosing a career?"

"In that I should be governed largely by the bent of each youth. What he likes to do best of all, that he should do; and he should try to do it better than anyone else. That is legitimate emulation. Let him devote his full energy to his work; with the provision, however, that he needs change or recreation more in proportion as he uses his brain more. The more muscular the work, if not too heavy, the more hours, is a good rule: the more brain work, the fewer hours. Children at school should not be expected to work so long or so hard as if engaged in manual labor. Temperament, too, should be considered. A highly organized, nervous person, like a racehorse, may display intense activity for a short time, but it should be followed by a long period of rest; while the phlegmatic person, like the ox or the draft horse, can go all day without injury."

EDUCATION

"I believe in education most thoroughly, and think no one can have too much knowledge, if properly digested. But in many of our colleges, I have often thought, not more than one in five is radically improved by the course. Most collegiates waste too much time in frivolity, and somehow there seems to be little restraining power in the college to prevent this. I agree that students should have self-restraint and application themselves, but, in the absence of these, the college should supply more compulsion than is now the rule."

APPRENTICES

"Do you favor reviving the old apprentice system for would-be mechanics?"

"Only in rare cases. As a rule, we have special machines now that do as perfect work as the market requires; some of them, indeed, better work than can be done by hand. A boy or man can soon learn to tend one of these, when he becomes, for ordinary purposes, a specialist. Very few shops now have apprentices. No rule, however, will apply to all, and it may still be best for one to serve an apprenticeship in a trade in which he wishes to advance beyond any predecessor or competitor."

PREPARE TO THE UTMOST: THEN DO YOUR BEST

"Is success dependent more upon ability or opportunity?"

"Of course, opportunity is necessary. You couldn't run a mammoth department store on the desert of Sahara. But, given the possibility, the right man can make his opportunity, and should do so, if it is not at hand, or does not come, after reasonable waiting. Even Napoleon had to wait for his. On the other hand, if there is no ability, none can display itself, and the best opportunity must pass by unimproved. The true way is to first develop your ability to the last ounce, and then you will be ready for your opportunity, when it comes, or to make one, if none offers."

PRESENT OPPORTUNITIES

"Is the chance for a youth as good as it was twenty-five or fifty years ago?"

"Yes, and no. In any country, as it becomes more thickly populated, the chance for purely individual enterprises is almost sure to diminish. One notices this more as he travels through other and older countries, where, far more than with us, boys follow in the footsteps of their fathers, generation after generation. But for those who are willing to adapt themselves to circumstances, the chance, today, at least from a pecuniary standpoint, is better than ever before, for those starting in life. There was doubtless more chance for the individual boat-builder, in the days of King Philip, when each Indian made his own canoe; but there is certainly more profit now for an employee of our firm of boat-builders."

NATURAL EXECUTIVE ABILITY

"Granted, however, that he can find employment, how do his chances of rising compare with those of your youth?"

"They still depend largely upon the individual. *Some seem to have natural executive ability, and others develop it, while most men never possess it. Those who lack it cannot hope to rise far, and never could.* Jefferson's idea that all men are created equal is true enough, perhaps, so far as their political rights are concerned, but from the point of view of efficiency in business, it is ridiculous. In any shop of one hundred men, you will find one who is acknowledged, at least tacitly, as the leader, and he sooner or later becomes so in fact. A rich boy may get and hold a place in an office, on account of his wealth or influence; but in the works, merit alone will enable a man to hold a place long."

THE DEVELOPMENT OF POWER

"But what is his chance of becoming a proprietor?"

"That is smaller, of course, as establishments grow larger and more valuable. It is all bosh for every man to expect to become a Vanderbilt or a Rockefeller, or to be President. But, in the long run, a man will still rise and prosper in almost exact proportion to his real value to the business world. He will rise or fall according to his ability."

"Can he develop ability?"

"Yes, to a certain extent. As I have said, we are not all alike, and no amount of cultivation will make some minds equal to those of others who have had but little training. But, whether great or small, everyone has some weak point; let him first study to overcome that."

"How can he do it?"

"The only way I know of is to—do it. But this brings me back to what I told you at first. A good mother will show one how to guard against his weak points. She should study each child and develop his individual character, for character is the true foundation, after all. She should check extravagance and encourage industry and self-respect. My mother is one of the best, and I feel I owe her a debt I can never repay."

"MY MOTHER"

"Your mother? Why, I thought you had been a boatbuilder for half a century! How old is she?"

"She is eighty-eight, and still enjoys good health. If I have one thing more than another to be thankful for, it is her care in childhood and her advice and sympathy through life. How often have I thought of her wisdom when I have seen mothers from Europe (where they were satisfied to be peasants), seek to outshine all their neighbors after they have been in America a few years, and so bring financial ruin to their husbands or even goad them into crime, and curse their children with contempt for honest labor in positions for which they are fitted, and a foolish desire to keep up appearances, even by living beyond their means and by seeking positions they cannot fill properly."

A BOAT BUILDER IN YOUTH

"You must have been quite young, when you began to build boats?"

"About thirteen or fourteen years old. You see, my father was an amateur boat-builder, in a small way, and did very good work, but usually not for sale. But I began the work as a business thirty-six years ago, when I was about twenty-two."

HE WOULD NOT BE DISCOURAGED

"You must have been terribly handicapped by your blindness."

"It was an obstacle, but I simply would not allow it to discourage me, and did my best, just the same as if I could see. My mother had taught me to think, and so I made thought and memory take the place of eyes. I acquired a kind of habit of mental projection which has enabled me to see models in my mind, as it were, and to consider their good and bad points intelligently. Besides, I cultivated my powers of observation to the utmost, in other respects. Even now, I take an occasional trip of observation, for I like to see what others are doing, and so keep abreast of the progress of the age. But I must stop or I shall get to 'talking shop,' the thing I declined to do at first.

THE SUM OF IT ALL

"The main thing for a boy is to have a good mother, to heed her advice, to do his best, and not get a 'swelled head' as he rises,—in other words, not to expect to put a gallon into a pint cup, or a bushel into a peck measure. Concentration, decision, industry and economy should be his watchwords, and invincible determination and persistence his rule of action."

With another cordial handshake, he bade me good-by.

II

WHAT THE HERRESHOFF BROTHERS HAVE BEEN DOING

Their recent Cup Defenders have made their names familiar to all, but shipping circles have long known them. The business of the firm was long confined almost wholly to the creation of boats with single masts, each craft from twenty to thirty-six feet long. In their first ten years of associated work, they built nearly two thousand of these. But they were wonderful little boats, and of unrivaled swiftness. Then they made as wonderful a success in building steam fishing yachts. Then came torpedo boats.

And in 1881 their proposal to the British government to build two vedette boats was accepted on condition they should outmatch the work of White, the naval launch builder at Cowes. No firm had ever been able to compete with White. But in the following July the two Herreshoff boats were in the Portsmouth dockyard, England, ready for trial. They were each forty-eight feet long, nine feet in beam, and five feet deep, exactly the same size as White's. They made fifteen and one-half knots an hour, while White's only recorded twelve and two-fifths knots. "With all their machinery coal and water in place. the Herreshoff boats were filled with water, and then twenty men were put aboard each, that human load being just so much in excess the admiralty test, and even then each had a floating capacity of three tons. The examiners pronounced enthusiastically in favor of the

The race between the "Vigilant" and the "Valkyrie."

(The "Vigilant," Herreshoff boat, the winner.)

Herreshoff safety coil boilers as unexplodable, less liable to injury from shock, capable of raising steam more quickly, far lighter, and in all respects superior to those that had been formerly used for the purpose." The boats were accepted, and orders given at once for two pinnaces, each thirty-three feet long. Again John Samuel White competed, but his new boats could only make seven and one-eighth knots, while the Herreshoff's easily scored nine and one-quarter.

RACING JAY GOULD

In July, 1883, Jay Gould was highly elated over the speed of his beautiful steam yacht "Atalanta," which had several times met and distanced Edward S. Jaffray's wonderful "Stranger;" but, on the twentieth of that month, his happiness, as the story is told, was very suddenly dashed.

After a hard day's work, the jaded Jay boarded the "Atalanta" and began to shake out his pin-feathers a little, figuratively speaking. But before his boat had gone far on her run to Irvington, the bold manipulator of Wall Street made out a craft on his weather-quarter that seemed to be gliding after the "Atalanta" with intent to overhaul her. He had a good start, however, and sang out to the captain to keep a sharp eye on the persistent little stranger, so unlike the "Stranger" he had vanquished.

"I wonder what it is!" he exclaimed to a friend beside him.

The friend looked long and carefully at the oncoming boat, then turned a quizzical eye on Jay, remarking:—

"In a little while we can tell."

"Will she get that close?"

"I think she will."

It was not long before the strange boat was abreast of the "Atalanta," and Jay was then able to make out the mystical number "100" on her. He rubbed his eyes. Those were the very figures he had long hoped to see on the stock ticker, after the words "Western Union," but that day they had lost their charm. Before long he was not only able to see the broadside of the "100," but also had a good view of the stern of the vessel, whereon the same figures soon appeared and nearly as soon disappeared, as the "100" bade good-by to the "Atalanta," which was burning every pound of coal that could possibly be carried without putting Mr. Gould or some efficient substitute on the safety valve.

"He seems to be out of humor to-night," said his coachman, after leaving his employer at the door of his Irvington mansion.

The mystic "100" which, by the way, was just one hundred feet over all, was merely the hundredth steamer built by the Herreshoffs, but on her first trip up the Hudson she attracted as much attention as the "Half Moon" of Henry Hudson or the "Clermont" of Robert Fulton. She was the fastest yacht in the world, and was beaten on the river by only one vessel, the "Mary Powell"—four and one-half minutes in twenty miles.

Although Mr. Gould was considerably irritated at his defeat, he knew a good thing when he saw it, and the next year he ordered a small steam launch of the Herreshoffs.

The "100" made a great stir in Boston Harbor. Later on she steamed through the Erie canal and the Great Lakes, and made her home with the millionaire Mark Hopkins.

THE "STILETTO"

The versatility of the Herreshoffs has appeared in their famous boiler improvement, and in the great variety of vessels they have built. The "Stiletto" only ninety-four feet long, over all, astonished the yachting world in 1885. On June 10, she beat the "Mary Powell" two miles in a race of twenty-eight miles on the Hudson. At one time, the "Stiletto" circled completely around the big steamer and then moved rapidly away, from her.

Secretary Whitney bought the "Stiletto" for the United States navy, in which she has done valuable service. She was followed, in 1890, by the still faster "Cushing," whose record in the recent Spanish-American war is so well known.

Admiral Porter wrote to Secretary of the Navy Chandler, that the little Herreshoff steam launches were faster than any other owned by the government, their great superiority showing especially against a strong head wind and sea. when they would remain dry while their rivals required constant bailing. They were better trimmed, lighter, more buoyant, and in every way superior in nautical qualities, and twice as fast as others in a gale.

Nineteen vessels have been built by this firm for the United States government.

"There is a certain speed that attaches to

every vessel, which may be called its natural rate," says Lewis Herreshoff; "it is mainly governed by its length and the length of the carrier wave which always accompanies a vessel parallel to her line of motion. When she reaches a speed great enough to form a wave of the same length as the moving body, then that vessel has reached her natural rate of speed, and all that can be obtained above that is done by sheer brute force. The natural limit of speed of a boat forty feet long is about ten miles an hour; of a vessel sixty feet in length, twelve and one-quarter miles; of one a hundred feet long, fifteen and three-fourths miles; of one two hundred feet long, twenty-two miles."

As the speed is increased, this double or carrier wave, one-half on either side of the yacht, lengthens in such a way that the vessel seems to settle more the faster she goes, and so has to climb the very wave she makes. Hence the motive power must be increased much faster than the speed increases. Further, in order to avoid this settling and consequent climbing as much as possible, lightness of construction, next to correct proportions, is made the great desideratum in the Herreshoffs' ideal boat. They use wood wherever possible, as it is not only lighter than metal, but is reasonably strong and generally much more durable. Wherever heavy strains come, a bracing form of construction is adopted, and metal is used also.

The engine of the "Stiletto" weighs ten pounds for each indicated horse-power; that of the "Cushing," fifteen. The entire motive plant of the "Cushing" weighs sixty-five pounds for each horse-power; that of the "City of Paris," two hundred. Comparing displacement, the former has eight times the power of the latter.

For four years our government kept a staff of officers stationed at the Herreshoff works to experiment with high-speed machinery, in which the firm then led the country. One of their steamers, ascending the St. Lawrence River to the Thousand Islands, ran up all the rapids except the Lachine, where a detour by canal was made. The Canadians were deeply impressed by this triumph.

THE BLIND BROTHERS

One of the Herreshoff sisters is blind and a remarkable musician; and one brother blind who studied music in Berlin, and who conducts a school of music in Providence. Lewis Herreshoff, one of the boat-builders, is also blind. He, too, is a fine musician and an excellent bass singer, having received careful vocal training in Europe. He has fine literary taste, a very clear style, and writes for magazines, especially on boat-building and engineering. He has a large foreign correspondence, all of which he answers personally on the typewriter. It would be difficult to find a greater favorite with young people, to whom he devotes much of his time, teaching them games or lessons, also how to sail or row a boat, how to swim or float, and how to save each other from drowning. When walking along the street with a group of chatting children, he will ask, "What time is it by the clock on St. Michael's Church?" pointing right at the steeple. He will wind a clock and set it exactly, and regulate it, if it does not go right.

THE PERSONALITY OF JOHN B. HERRESHOFF

From his boyhood, John B. Herreshoff evinced a great fondness for boats and machinery, finding most pleasure, in his leisure hours, when boys of his age usually think only of play, in haunting boat-builders' yards and machine shops, studying how and why things were done, and reading what had been done elsewhere in those branches of industry, beyond his field of observation.

At the age of eleven, he was studying the best lines for vessels' hulls and making models and three years later he began building boats.

His terrible affliction has never seemed to weaken his self-reliance or turn him aside from following the chosen pursuit of his life, but has rather strengthened his devotion to it and his capacity for it by concentrating all his faculties upon it.

His many years of blindness have given him not only the serious, patient, introspective look common to those who suffer like him, and their gentle, clearly modulated voice, but have also developed all his other faculties to such an extent as to largely replace the missing sense.

He can tell as much about an ordinary-sized steam launch, her lines, methods of construction, etc., by feeling, as others can by seeing, and he goes on inventing and building just as if his eyes were not closed forever. He is a tall, big-brained man, who couldn't help inventing and working if he tried. Such a man would have to suffer the loss of more than one of his senses before his mental efficiency would be impaired. When he wanted to build some steam launches for the government, he went to the navy yard at Washington and felt of the government launches, to discover their shape and how they were made. Then he went to Bristol and made better launches suitable for the government's use.

HAS HE A SIXTH SENSE?

He reads and understands the most delicate intonations and modulations of voices addressing him, as others read and understand facial expression. His sensitive fingers detect differences in metals, and follow, as if with a gift of perception, the lines of models submitted to him, and his mind sees even more clearly than by mere physical sight the intricacies of the most complicated machinery intelligently described to him, or over which his fingers are allowed to move. "That is a good stick," he will say, examining a pile of lumber with his fingers. "Here's a shaky piece, throw it out; it won't do for this work," may come next, or, "Saw off this end; it's poor stock. The rest is all right." On hearing him criticize, direct, and explain things within his province, a stranger finds it hard to believe he cannot see at least a little,—out of one eye.

SEEING WITH THE FINGERS

By the constant practice, he has, as he expresses it, learned to see with his hands, not quite so quickly, but he believes as perfectly, as he could with his eyes, and this means more than it does in the case of an ordinary blind man; for, by a touch, he can tell whether the graceful double curves of a boat's bottom are in correct proportion, one with another, and then, by a few rapid sweeps of his hands, over all, he can instantly judge of the symmetry and perfection of the whole. Even more than this, he will give minute directions to the carpenters and mechanics, running his hand along the piece of work one had produced, will immediately detect the slightest deviation from the instruction he has given. If at all impatient, he will seize the plane or other tool, and do the work himself. And yet the world calls this man "blind!"

While skill plays a material part, one of John B. Herreshoff's boats is a product of the mind, in a very great degree. Psychologists tell us that we do not see with our eyes, but with the brain proper. This blind man sees, and constructs, not that which is objective and real to others, but that which is evolved from a transcendental intelligence applied to the most practical purposes.

BROTHER NAT

One of the brothers, who has good eyes, is a prominent chemist in New York; and one who can see is Nat the designer for the boat-building.

Nathaniel G., the great yacht designer, was born in 1848. When he was not more than two years old, he was often found asleep on the sand along shore, with the rising tide washing his bare feet. Whenever he was missing, he was sought for first on the shore, where he would generally be found watching the ships or playing with toy boats.

At nine years of age, he was an excellent helmsman, and at twelve he sailed the "Sprite" to her first victory and won a prize. When older grown, he was known as a vigilant watcher of every chance as well as a skillful sailor. Once, when steering the "Ianthe" in a failing wind, he veered widely from a crowd of contestants, so as to run into a good breeze he noted far to starboard, and won the race.

He took a four years' course at the Massachusetts Institute of Technology, and then served an apprenticeship with the famous Corliss Engine Company. He worked on the great engine at the Centennial Exposition, and took a course of engineering abroad, visiting many noted shipyards. He joined the firm in 1877, fourteen years after the works were opened.

Nathaniel Greene Herreshoff, named for General Greene of Revolutionary fame, is seven years younger, and only less famous than his blind brother as a boat-builder,—only second to John B. in about the same way that Greene was second to Washington. "General Greene is second to no one," said Washington. John B. would have done splendid work without Nat as he did for years before the latter joined the firm, but it would have been in a smaller way.

For years John B., his father, and his brothers, James B. or Lewis, and Nathaniel G., were accustomed to get together frequently in the dining-room of the old homestead, and talk and plan together in regard to boat-building. Nat would usually make the first model on lines previously agreed upon, and then John B.

would feel it over and suggest changes, which would be made, and the consultation continued until all was satisfactory.

Nathaniel is described as "a tall, thin man, with a full beard and a stoop," the latter said to have been acquired in "watching his rivals in his races, craning his head in order to see them from under the boom."

"We have been always together from boyhood," said John B., speaking of "Nat;" "we have had the same pleasures, the same purposes, the same aspirations; in fact, we have almost been one, and we have achieved nothing for which a full share of credit is not his just due. Nothing has ever been done by one without the other. Whenever one found an obstacle or difficulty, the other helped him to remove it; and he, being without the disadvantage I have, never makes a mistake."

XVIII

A Successful Novelist: Fame After Fifty[1]

Practical Hints to Young Authors,

BY MRS. AMELIA E. BARR

TO be successful! That is the legitimate ideal every true worker seeks to realize. But success is not the open secret which it appears to be; its elements are often uncomprehended; and its roots generally go deep down, into the very beginnings of life. I can compel my soul to look back into that twilight which shrouds my earliest years, and perceive, even in them, monitions and tendencies working for that future, which in my des-

[1] This is a most remarkable story, communicated to me by Mrs. Barr, and related for the first time in this article. The distinguished novelist, being a perfect housekeeper and the mother of a large family, yet earns $20,000 a year by her books, which have been translated into the language of almost every civilized country.—O. S. M.

tiny was fashioned and shaped when as yet there was neither hint nor dream of it. Fortunately, I had parents who understood the

VALUE OF BIBLICAL AND IMAGINATIVE LITERATURE

in the formation of the intellect. The men and women whom I knew first and best were those of the Hebrew world. Sitting before the nursery fire, while the snow fell softly and ceaselessly, and all the mountains round were white, and the streets of the little English town choked with drifts, I could see the camels and the caravans of the Ishmaelitish merchants, passing through the hot, sandy desert. I could see Hagar weeping under the palm, and the waters of the Red Sea standing up like a wall. Miriam clashing the timbrels, and Deborah singing under the oak, and Ruth gleaning in the wheatfields of Bethlehem, were as real to me as were the women of my own home. Before I was six years old, I had been with Christian to the Celestial City, and had watched, with Crusoe, the mysterious footprint on the sand, and the advent of the savages. Then came the wonders of afrites and genii, and all the marvels and miracles of the Arabian tales.

These were the mind-builders, and though schools and teachers and text-books did much afterwards, I can never nor will forget the glorious company of men and women from the sacred world, and that marvelous company of caliphs and kings and princesses from Wonder Land and Fairy Land, that expanded my whole nature, and fitted me for the future miracles of Nature and Science, and all the marvelous people of the Poet's realm.

For eighteen years I was amassing facts and fancies, developing a crude intelligence, waiting for the vitalization of the heart. Then Love, the Supreme Teacher, came; and his first lesson was,

RENUNCIATION.

I was to give up father, and mother, home and kindred, friends and country, and follow where he would lead me, into a land strange and far off. Child-bearing and child-losing; the limitations and delights of frontier life; the intimate society of such great and individual men as Sam Houston, and the men who fought with him; the intense feelings induced by war, its uncertainties and possibilities, and the awful abiding in the Valley of the Shadow of Death, with the pestilence that walked in darkness and the sickness that destroyed at noonday;—all these events with their inevitable "asides" were instrumental in the education and preparation of the seventeen years of my married life.

The calamitous lesson of widowhood, under peculiarly tragic circumstances, was the last initiation of a heart already broken and humbled before Him who doeth all things well, no matter how hard the stroke may be. I thought all was over then; yet all was just beginning. It was the open door to a new life—a life full of comforts, and serene, still,

DELIGHTFUL STUDIES.

Though I had written stories to please my children, and many things to please myself, it had never occurred to me that money could be made by writing. The late William Libbey, a man of singular wisdom and kindness, first made me understand that my brain and my ten fingers were security for a good living. From my first effort I began to gather in the harvest of all my years of study and reading and private writing. For there is this peculiarity about writing—that if in any direction it has merit, it will certainly find a market.

For fifteen years I wrote short stories, poems, editorials, and articles on every conceivable subject, from Herbert Spencer's theories, to gentlemen's walking sticks; but bringing to every piece of work, if it was only ten lines, the best of my knowledge and ability; and so earning, with a great deal of pleasure, a very good living. During the earlier years of this time I worked and read on an average

FIFTEEN HOURS A DAY;

for I knew that, to make good work, I must have constant fresh material; must keep up to date in style and method; and must therefore *read* far more than I wrote. But I have been an omnivorous reader all my life long, and no changes, no cares of home and children, have ever interfered with this mental necessity. In the most unlikely places and circumstances, I looked for books, and found them. These fifteen years on the weekly and monthly periodicals gave me the widest opportunities for information. I had an alcove in the Astor Library, and I practically lived in it. I slept and ate at home, but I lived in that City of

Books. I was in the prime of life, but neither society, amusements, nor pleasures of any kind, could draw me away from the source of all my happiness and profit.

Suddenly, after this long novition, I received the "call" for a different work. I had

AN ACCIDENT

which confined me to my room, and which, I knew, would keep me from active work for some months. I fretted for my work, as dry wood frets an inch from the flame, and said, "I shall lose all I have gained; I shall fall behind in the race; all these things are against me." They were all for me. A little story of what seemed exceptional merit, had been laid away, in the hope that I might some day find time to extend it into a novel. A prisoner in my chair, I finished the book in six weeks, and sent it to Dodd, Mead & Co. On Thanksgiving morning, a letter came, accepting the book, and any of my readers can imagine what a happy Thanksgiving Day that was! This book was "Jan Vedder's Wife," and its great and immediate success indicated to me the work I was at length ready for. I was then in my fifty-second year, and every year had been a preparation for the work I have since pursued. I went out from that sick room sure of my

VOCATION;

and, with a confidence founded on the certainty of my equipment, and a determination to trust humanity, and take my readers only into green pastures and ways of purity and heroism, I ventured on my new path as a novelist.

I cannot close this paper without a few words to those who wish to profit by it. I want them to be sure of a few points which, in my narrative, I may not have emphasized sufficiently.

WORDS OF COUNSEL

1. Men and women succeed *because they take pains to succeed.* Industry and patience are almost genius; and successful people are often more distinguished for resolution and perseverance than for unusual gifts. They make determination and unity of purpose supply the place of ability.

2. Success is the reward of those who "spurn delights and live laborious days." We learn to do things by *doing them. One of the great secrets of success is "pegging away."*

No disappointment must discourage, and a run back must often be allowed, in order to take a longer leap forward.

3. *No opposition must be taken to heart.* Our enemies often help us more than our friends. Besides, a head-wind is better than no wind. Who ever got anywhere in a dead calm?

4. *A fatal mistake is to imagine that success is some stroke of luck.* This world is run with far too tight a rein for luck to interfere. Fortune *sells* her wares; she never gives them. In some form or other, we pay for her favors; or we go empty away.

5. We have been told, for centuries, to watch for opportunities, and to strike while the iron is hot. Very good; but I think better of Oliver Cromwell's amendment.—"*make the iron hot by striking it.*"

6. Everything good needs time. Don't do work in a hurry. Go into details; it pays in every way. *Time means power for your work.* Mediocrity is always in a rush; but whatever is worth doing at all is worth doing with consideration. For genius is nothing more nor less than doing well what anyone can do badly.

7. *Be orderly.* Slatternly work is never

good work. It is either affectation, or there is some radical defect in the intellect. I would distrust even the spiritual life of one whose methods and work were dirty, untidy, and without clearness and order.

8. Never be above your profession. I have had many letters from people who wanted all the emoluments and honors of literature, and who yet said, "Literature is the accident of my life; I am a lawyer, or a doctor, or a lady, or a gentleman." *Literature is no accident. She is a mistress who demands the whole heart, the whole intellect, and the whole time of a devotee.*

9. Don't fail through defects of temper and over-sensitiveness at moments of trial. *One of the great helps to success is to be cheerful;* to go to work with a full sense of life; to be determined to put hindrances out of the way; to prevail over them and to get the mastery. *Above all things else, be cheerful;* there is no beatitude for the despairing.

Apparent success may be reached by sheer impudence, in defiance of offensive demerit. But men who get what they are manifestly unfit for, are made to feel what people think of them. Charlatanry may flourish; but when its bay tree is greenest, it is held far lower than genuine effort. The world is just; it may, it does, patronize quacks; but *it never puts them on a level with true men.*

It is better to have the opportunity of victory, than to be spared the struggle; for success comes but as the result of arduous experience. The foundations of my success were laid before I can well remember; *it was after at least forty-five years of conscious labor that I reached the object of my hope.* Many a time my head failed me, my hands failed me, my feet failed me, but, thank God, my *heart* never failed me. Because *I knew that no extremity would find God's arm shortened.*

XIX

How Theodore Thomas Brought the People Nearer to Music

MR. THOMAS is an early riser, and as I found him one morning, in his chambers in Chicago, he was preparing to leave for rehearsal. The hale old gentleman actively paced the floor, while I conversed with him.

"Mr. Thomas," I said, "those familiar with the events of your life consider them a lesson of encouragement for earnest and high-minded artists."

"That is kind," he answered.

"I should like, if you will, to have you speak of your work in building up your great orchestra in this country."

"That is too long a story. I would have to begin with my birth."

"Where were you born?" I asked.

"In the kingdom of Hanover, in 1835. My father was a violinist, and from him I inherited my taste, I suppose. He taught me music. When I was only six years old, I played the violin at public concerts.

"I WAS NOT AN INFANT PRODIGY"

"I was not an infant prodigy, however. My father had too much wisdom to injure my chances in that way. He made me keep to my studies in a manner that did me good. I came to America in 1845."

"Was the American music field crowded then?"

"On the contrary, there wasn't any field to speak of. It had to be made. Music was the pastime of a few. The well-educated and fashionable classes possessed or claimed a knowledge of it. There was scarcely any music for the common people."

"How did you get your start in the New York world of music?" I asked.

"With four associates, William Mason, Joseph Mosenthal, George Matzka and Frederick Berguer, I began a series of concerts of Chamber Music, and for many years we conducted this modest artistic enterprise. There was much musical enthusiasm on our part, but very little reward, except the pleasure we drew from our own playing.

"These Mason and Thomas *soirées* are still remembered by old-time music lovers of New York, not only for their excellence, but for the peculiar character of the audiences. They were quiet little monthly reunions, to which most of the guests came with complimentary tickets. The critics hardly ventured to intrude upon the exercises, and the newspapers gave them little notice."

BEGINNING OF THE ORCHESTRA

"How did you come to found your great orchestra?"

"It was more of a growth than a full-fledged thought to begin with. It was in 1861 that I severed my connection with the opera and began to establish a genuine orchestra. I began with occasional performances, popular matinée concerts, and so on, and, in a few years, was able to give a series of Symphony *Soirées* at the old Irving Hall in New York."

To the average person this work of Mr. Thomas may seem to be neither difficult nor great. Yet while anyone could have collected a band in a week, to make such an orchestra as Mr. Thomas meant to have, required time and patience. It was when the Philharmonic Society, after living through a great many hardships, was on the full tide of popular favor. Its concerts and rehearsals filled the Academy of Music with the flower of New York society. Powerful social influences had been won to its support, and Carl Bergmann had raised its noble orchestra of one hundred performers to a point of proficiency then quite unexampled in this country, and in some particulars still unsurpassed. Ladies and gentlemen who moved in the best circles hardly noticed the parallel entertainment offered in such a modest way, by Mr. Thomas, on the opposite side of the street. The patrons of his Chamber Concerts, of course, went in to see what the new orchestra was like; professional musicians hurried to the hall with their free passes; and there were a few curious listeners besides who found in the programmes a class of compositions somewhat different from those which Mr. Bergmann chiefly favored, and, in particular, a freshness and novelty in the selections, with an inclination, not yet very strongly marked, toward the modern German school. Among such of the *dilettanti* as condescended to think of Mr. Thomas at all, there was a vague impression that his concerts were started in opposition to the Philharmonic Society, but that they were not so good and much less genteel.

It is true that Mr. Thomas was surpassed, at that time, by Mr. Bergmann's larger and older orchestra, and that he had much less than an equal share of public favor, but there was no intentional rivalry. The two men had entirely different ideas and worked them out in perfectly original ways. It was only the artist's dismal period of struggle and neglect, which every beginner must pass through. He had to meet cold and meager audiences, and the false judgment of both the critics and the people. Yet he was a singular compound of good American energy and German obstinacy, and he never lost courage.

"Was it a long struggle?" I asked.

"Not very long. Matters soon began to mend. The orchestra improved, the dreadful gaps in the audience soon filled up, and at the end of the year the Symphony *Soirées,* if they made no excitement in musical circles, had at least achieved a high reputation."

"What was your aim, at that time?"

"When I began, I was convinced that there is no music too high for the popular appreciation,—that no scientific education is required for the enjoyment of Beethoven. I believed that it is only necessary that a public whose taste has been vitiated by over-indulgence in trifles, should have time and opportunity to accustom itself to better things. The American people at large then (1864) knew little or nothing of the great composers for the orchesstra. Three or four more or less complete organizations had visited the principal cities of the United States in former years, but they made little permanent impression. Juillien had brought over, for his monster concerts, only five or six solo players, and the band was filled up with such material as he found here. The celebrated Germania Band of New York, which had first brought Mr. Bergmann (famous then as the head of the New York Philharmonic Society) into notice, did some admirable work just previous to my start in New York, but it disbanded after six years of vicissitude, and, besides, it was not a complete orchestra."

"You mean," I said, as Mr. Thomas paused meditatively, "that you came at a time when there was a decided opportunity?"

MUSIC HAD NO HOLD ON THE MASSES

"Yes. There had been, and were then, good organizations, such as the New York Philharmonic Society and the Harvard Musical Association in Boston, and a few similar organizations in various parts of the country. I mean no disparagement to their honorable labors, but, in simple truth, none of them had great influence on the masses. They were pioneers of culture. They prepared the way for the modern permanent orchestra."

"They were not important?"

"No, no; that cannot be said. It would be the grossest ingratitude to forget what they did and have done and are still doing, or detract in the smallest degree from their well-earned fame. But from the very nature of their organization, it was inevitable that they should stand a little apart from the common crowd. To the general public, their performances were more like mysterious rites, celebrated behind closed doors, in the presence of a select and unchanging company of believers. Year after year, the same twenty-five hundred people filled the New York Academy of Music at the Philharmonic concerts, applauding the same class of master works, and growing more and more familiar with the same standards of the strictly classical school. This was no cause for complaint; on the contrary, it was most fortunate that the reverence for the older forms of art and canons of taste were thus kept alive; and we know that, little by little, the culture which the Philharmonic Society diffuses, through the circle of its regular subscribers, spreads beyond that small company, and raises the æsthetic tone of metropolitan life. But I believed then, as I believe now, that it would require generations for this little leaven to leaven the whole mass, and so I undertook to do my part in improving matters by forming an orchestra."

"You wanted to get nearer the people with good music?"

"No, I wanted the people to get nearer to music. I was satisfied that the right course is to begin at the bottom instead of the top, and make the cultivation of symphonic music a popular movement."

"Was the idea of a popular permanent orchestra new at that time?"

"Yes."

"Why was it necessary to effect a permanent orchestra?"

"Why? Because the first step in making music popular was to raise the standard of orchestral performances and increase their frequency. Our country had never possessed a genuine orchestra, for a band of players gathered together at rare intervals for a special purpose does not deserve the name. The musician who marches at the head of a target company all the morning and plays for a dancing party at night, is out of tune with the great masters. To express the deep emotions of Beethoven, the romanticism of Schumann, or the poetry of Liszt, he ought to live in an atmosphere of art, and keep not only his hand in practice, but his mind properly attempered. An orchestra, therefore, ought to be a permanent body, whose members play together every day, under the same conductor, and devote themselves exclusively to genuine music. Nobody had yet attempted to found an orchestra of this kind in America when I began; but I believed it could be done."

WORKING OUT HIS IDEA

"Did you have an idea of a permanent building for your orchestra?"

"Yes. I wanted something more than an ordinary concert-room. The idea needed it. It was to be a place suitable for use at all seasons of the year. There was to be communication in summer with an open garden, and in winter it was to be a perfect auditorium."

Mr. Thomas's idea went even further. It must be bright, comfortable, roomy, well ventilated—for a close and drowsy atmosphere is fatal to symphonic music,—it must offer to the multitude every attraction not inconsistent with musical enjoyment. The stage must be adapted for a variety of performances, for popular summer entertainment as well as the most serious of classical concerts. There, with an uninterrupted course of entertainments, night after night, the whole year round, the noblest work of all the great masters might be worthily presented.

The scheme was never wholly worked out in New York, great as Mr. Thomas's fame became, but it was partially realized in the old Exposition building in Chicago, where he afterwards gave his summer concerts, and it is still nearer reality in the present permanent Chicago orchestra, which has the great Auditorium for its home and a $50,000 annual guarantee.

"What were your first steps in this direction?" I asked.

"I began with a series of *al fresco* entertainments in the old Terrace Garden, in June, 1866. They were well patronized; and repeated in 1867. Then, in 1868, we removed to better quarters in Central Park Garden, and things prospered, so that, in 1869, I began those annual tours, which are now so common."

The first itinerary of this kind was not very profitable, but the young conductor fought through it. Each new season improved somewhat, but there were troubles and losses. More than once, the travelers trod close upon the heels of calamity. The cost of moving from place to place was so great that the most careful management was necessary to cover expenses. They could not afford to be idle, even for a night, and the towns capable of furnishing good audiences generally wanted fun. Hence they must travel all day, and Thomas took care that the road should be smoothed with all obtainable comforts. Special cars on the railways, special attendants to look after the luggage, and lodgings at the best hotels contributed to make the tour tolerably pleasant and easy, so that the men came to their evening work fresh and smiling. They were tied up by freshets and delayed by wrecks; but their fame grew, and the audiences became greater. Thomas's fame as a conductor who could guarantee constant employment permitted him to take his choice of the best players in the country, and he brought over a number of European celebrities as the public taste improved.

Theodore Thomas did another wise thing. He treated New York like a provincial city, giving it a week of music once in a while as he passed through it on his travels. This excited the popular interest, and when he came to stay, the next season, a brilliantly successful series of concerts was the result. At the close, a number of his admirers united in presenting him a rich silver casket, holding a purse of thirty-five hundred dollars, as a testimonial of gratitude for his services. The Brooklyn Philharmonic Society placed itself under his direction. Chicago gave him a fine invitation to attend benefit entertainments to himself; and, when he came, decked the hall with abundant natural flowers, as if for the reception of a hero. He was successful financially and every other way, and from that time on he merely added to his laurels.

THE CHIEF ELEMENT OF HIS SUCCESS

"What," I asked of him, "do you consider the chief element of your success?"

"That is difficult to say. Perseverance, hard work, stern discipline,—each had its part."

"You have never attempted to become rich?"

"Poh!"

"Do you still believe in the best music for the mass of the people?"

"I do. My success has been with them. It was so in New York; it is so here in Chicago."

"Do you still work as hard as ever?" I inquired.

"Nearly so. The training of a large orchestra never ends. The work must be gone over and over. There is always something new."

"And your life's pleasure lies in this?"

"Wholly so. To render perfect music perfectly—that is enough."

XX

John Burroughs at Home: The Hut on the Hill Top

WHEN I visited the hill-top retreat of John Burroughs, the distinguished writer upon nature, at West Park, New York, it was with the feeling that all success is not material; that mere dollars are nothing, and that the influential man is the successful man, whether he be rich or poor. John Burroughs is unquestionably both influential and poor. Relatively poor: being an owner of some real estate, and having a modest income from copyrights. He is content: knowing when he has enough. On the wooden porch of his little bark-covered cabin I waited, one June afternoon, until he should come back from the woods and fields, where he had gone for a ramble. It was so still that the sound of my rocker moving to and fro on the rough boards of the little porch seemed to shock the perfect quiet.

From afar off came the plaintive cry of a wood-dove, and then all was still again. Presently the interpreter of out-door life appeared in the distance, and, seeing a stranger at his door, hurried homeward. He was without coat or vest and looked cool in his white outing shirt and large straw hat. After some formalities of introduction we reached the subject which I had called to discuss, and he said:—

"It is not customary to interview men of my vocation concerning success."

"Any one who has made a lasting impression on the minds of his contemporaries," I began, "and influenced men and women—"

"Do you refer to me?" he interrupted, naïvely.

I nodded and he laughed. "I have not endowed a university nor made a fortune, nor conquered an enemy in battle," he said.

"And those who have done such things have not written 'Locusts and Wild Honey' and 'Wake Robin.'"

"I recognize," he said quietly, "that success is not always where people think it is. There are many ways of being successful; and I do not approve of the mistake which causes many to consider that a great fortune acquired means a great success achieved. On the contrary, our greatest men need very little money to accomplish the greatest work."

"I thought that anyone leading a life so wholly at variance with the ordinary ideas and customs would see success in life from a different point of view," I observed. "Money is really no object with you?"

"The subject of wealth never disturbs me."

"You lead a very simple life here."

"Such as you see."

The sight would impress anyone. So far is this disciple of nature away from the ordinary mode of the world, that his little cabin, set in the cup-shaped top of a hill, is practically bare of luxuries and the so called comforts of life. His surroundings are of the rudest, the very rocks and bushes encroaching upon his back door. All about, the crest of the hill encircles him, and shuts out the world. Only the birds of the air venture to invade his retreat from the various sides of the mountain; and there is only one approach by a straggling, narrow path. In his house are no decorations but such as can be hung upon the exposed wood. The fireplace is of brick, and quite wide; the floor, rough boards scrubbed white; the ceiling, a rough array of exposed rafters; and his bed rudely constructed. Very few and very simple chairs, a plain table and some shelves for books make the wealth of the retreat and serve for his ordinary use.[1]

"Many people," I said, "think that your method of living is an ideal example of the way people ought to live."

"There is nothing remarkable in that. A great many people are very weary of the way they think themselves compelled to live. They are mistaken in believing that the disagreeable things they find themselves doing, are the things they ought to do. A great many take their ideas of a proper aim in life from what other people say and do. Consequently, they are unhappy, and an independent existence such as mine strikes them as ideal. As a matter of fact, it is very natural."

"Would you say that to work so as to be

[1] This hut on the hill-top is situated in an old lake bed, some three hundred yards wide, half filled with peat and decomposed matter, swampy and overgrown. This area was devoted by Mr. Burroughs to the raising of celery for the market, when he set out to earn a living upon the land.

able to live like this should be the aim of a young man?"

"By no means. On the contrary, his aim should be to live in such a way as will give his mind the greatest freedom and peace. This can be very often obtained by wanting less of material things and more of intellectual ones. A man who achieved such an aim would be as well off as the most distinguished man in any field. Money-getting is half a mania, and some other 'getting' propensities are manias also. The man who gets content comes nearest to being reasonable."

"I should like," I said, "to illustrate your point of view from the details of your own life."

"Students of nature do not, as a rule, have eventful lives. I was born at Roxbury, New York, in 1837. That was a time when conditions were rather primitive. My father was a farmer, and I was raised among the woods and fields. I came from an uncultivated, unreading class of society, and grew up among surroundings the least calculated to awaken the literary faculty. I have no doubt that daily contact with the woods and fields awakened my interest in the wonders of nature, and gave me a bent toward investigation in that direction."[1]

"Did you begin early to make notes and write upon nature?" I questioned.

"Not before I was sixteen or seventeen. Earlier than that, the art of composition had anything but charms for me. I remember that while at school, at the age of fourteen, I was required, like other students, to write 'compositions' at stated times, but I usually evaded the duty one way or another. On one occasion, I copied something from a comic almanac, and unblushingly handed it in as my own. But the teacher detected the fraud, and ordered me to produce a twelve-line composition before I left school. I remember I racked my brain in vain,

[1] "Blessed is he whose youth was passed upon a farm," writes Mr. Burroughs; "and if it was a dairy farm his memories will be all the more fragrant. The driving of the cows to and from the pasture every day and every season for years,—how much of summer and of nature he got into him on these journeys! What rambles and excursions did this errand furnish the excuse for! The birds and birds' nests, the berries, the squirrels, the woodchucks, the beech woods into which the cows loved so to wander and browse, the fragrant wintergreens. and a hundred nameless adventures, all strung upon that brief journey of half a mile to and from the remote pasture."

and the short winter day was almost closing when Jay Gould, who sat in the seat behind me, wrote twelve lines of doggerel on his slate and passed it slyly over to me. I had so little taste for writing that I coolly copied that, and handed it in as my own."

"You were friendly with Gould then?"

"Oh, yes, 'chummy,' they call it now. His father's farm was only a little way from ours, and we were fast friends, going home together every night."

"His view of life must have been considerably different from yours."

"It was. I always looked upon success as being a matter of mind, not money; but Jay wanted the material appearances. I remember that once we had a wrestling match, and as we were about even in strength, we agreed to abide by certain rules,—taking what we called 'holts' in the beginning and not breaking them until one or the other was thrown. I kept to this in the struggle, but when Jay realized that he was in danger of losing the contest, he broke the 'holt' and threw me. When I remarked that he had broken his agreement, he only laughed and said, 'I threw you, didn't I?' And to every objection I made, he made the same answer. The fact of having won was pleasing to him. It satisfied him, although it wouldn't have contented me."

"Did you ever talk over success in life with him?"

"Yes, quite often. He was bent on making money, and did considerable trading among us schoolboys,—sold me some of his books. I felt then that my view of life was more satisfactory to me than his would have been. I wanted to obtain a competence, and then devote myself to high thinking instead of to money-making.[1]

"How did you plan to attain this end?"

"By study. I began in my sixteenth or seventeenth year to try to express myself on paper, and when, after I had left the country school, I attended the seminary at Ashland and at Cooperstown, I often received the highest

[1] An old schoolmate in the little red schoolhouse has said, that "John and Jay were not like the other boys. They learned their lessons easier; and at recess they looked on the games, but did not join in them. John always knew where to find the largest trout; he could show you birds' nests, and name all the flowers. He was fond of reading, and would walk five miles to borrow a book. Roxbury is proud of John Burroughs. We celebrated 'Burroughs Day' instead of Arbor Day here last spring, in the high-school, in honor of him."

marks in composition, though only standing about the average in general scholarship. My taste ran to essays, and I picked up the great works in that field at a bookstore, from time to time, and filled my mind with the essay idea. I bought the whole of Dr. Johnson's works at a second-hand bookstore in New York, because, on looking into them I found his essays appeared to be solid literature, which I thought was just the thing. Almost my first literary attempts were moral reflections, somewhat in the Johnsonian style."

"You were supporting yourself during these years?"

"I taught six months and 'boarded round' before I went to the seminary. That put fifty dollars into my pocket, and the fifty paid my way at the seminary.[1] Working on the farm,

---

[1] It was when he was attending the academy, that young Burroughs first saw that wonderful being—a living author:—

"I distinctly remember with what emotion I gazed upon him," he said, "and followed him about in the twilight, keeping on the other side of the street. He was of little account,—a man who had failed as a lawyer, and then had written a history of Poland, which I have never heard of since that time; but to me he was the embodiment of the august spirit of authorship, and I looked upon him with more reverence and enthusiasm

studying and teaching filled up the years until 1863, when I went to Washington and found employment in the Treasury Department."

"You were connected with the Treasury then?"[1]

"Oh, yes; for nearly nine years. I left the department in 1872, to become receiver of a bank, and subsequently for several years I performed the work of a bank examiner. I considered it only as an opportunity to earn and save up a little money on which I could retire. I managed to do that, and came back to this region, where I bought a fruit farm. I worked

---

than I had ever before looked upon any man with. I cannot divine why I should have stood in such worshipful fear and awe of this obscure individual, but I suppose it was the instinctive tribute of a timid and imaginative youth to a power he was just beginning to see,—or to feel,—the power of letters."

[1] "My first book, 'Wake-Robin,' was written while I was a government clerk in Washington," says Mr. Burroughs. "It enabled me to live over again the days I had passed with the birds, and in the scenes of my youth. I wrote the book while sitting at a desk in front of an iron wall. I was the keeper of a vault in which many million of bank-notes were stored. During my long periods of leisure, I took refuge in my pen. How my mind reacted from the iron wall in front of me, and sought solace in memories of the birds and of summer fields and woods."

that into paying condition, and then gave all my time to the pursuit of the studies I like."

"Had you abandoned your interest in nature during your Washington life?"

"No. I gave as much time to the study of nature and literature as I had to spare. When I was twenty-three I wrote an essay on 'Expression,' and sent it to the '*Atlantic.*' It was so Emersonian in style, owing to my enthusiasm for Emerson at that time, that the editor thought some one was trying to palm off on him an early essay of Emerson's which he had not seen. He found that Emerson had not published any such paper, however, and printed it, though it had not much merit. I wrote off and on for the magazines."

The editor in question was James Russell Lowell, who, instead of considering it without merit, often expressed afterwards the delight with which he read this contribution from an unknown hand, and the swift impression of the author's future distinction which came to him with that reading.

"Your successful work, then, has been in what direction?" I said.

"In studying nature. It has all come by living close to the plants and animals of the woods and fields, and coming to understand them. There I have been successful. Men who, like myself, are deficient in self-assertion, or whose personalities are flexible and yielding, make a poor show in business, but in certain other fields these defects become advantages. Certainly it is so in my case. I can succeed with bird or beast, for I have cultivated my ability in that direction. I can look in the eye of an ugly dog or cow and win, but with an ugly man I have less success.

"I consider the desire which most individuals have for the luxuries which money can buy, an error of mind" he added. "Those things do not mean anything except a lack of higher tastes. Such wants are not necessary wants, nor honorable wants. If you cannot get wealth with a noble purpose, it is better to abandon it and get something else. Peace of mind is one of the best things to seek, and finer tastes and feelings. The man who gets these, and maintains himself comfortably, is much more admirable and successful than the man who gets money and neglects these. The realm of power has no fascination for me. I would rather have my seclusion and peace of mind. This log hut, with its bare floors, is sufficient.

I am set down among the beauties of nature, and in no danger of losing the riches that are scattered all about. No one will take my walks or my brook away from me. The flowers, birds and animals are plentifully provided. I have enough to eat and wear, and time to see how beautiful the world is, and to enjoy it. The entire world is after your money, or the things you have bought with your money. It is trying to keep them that makes them seem so precious. I live to broaden and enjoy my own life, believing that in so doing I do what is best for everyone. If I ran after birds only to write about them, I should never have written anything that anyone else would have cared to read. I must write from sympathy and love,—that is, from enjoyment,—or not at all. I come gradually to have a feeling that I want to write upon a given theme. Whenever the subject recurs to me, it awakens a warm, personal response. My confidence that I ought to write comes from the feeling or attraction which some subjects exercise over me. The work is pleasure, and the result gives pleasure."

"And your work as a naturalist is what?"

"Climbing trees to study birds, lying by the waterside to watch the fishes, sitting still in the grass for hours to study the insects, and tramping here and there, always to observe and study whatever is common to the woods and fields."

"Men think you have done a great work," I said.

"I have done a pleasant work," he said, modestly.

"And the achievements of your schoolmate Gould do not appeal to you as having anything in them worth aiming for?" I questioned.

"Not for me. I think my life is better for having escaped such vast and difficult interests."

The gentle, light-hearted naturalist and recluse came down the long hillside with me, "to put me right" on the main road. I watched him as he retraced his steps up the steep, dark path, lantern in hand. His sixty years sat lightly upon him, and as he ascended I heard him singing. Long after the light melody had died away, I saw the serene little light bobbing up and down in his hand, disappearing and reappearing, as the lone philosopher repaired to his hut and his couch of content.

XXI

Vreeland's Romantic Story: How He Came to Transport a Million Passengers a Day

A SHORT time ago, New York learned with interest and some astonishment, that the head of its greatest transportation system, Herbert H. Vreeland, had received from several of his associates as individuals, a "valentine" present of $100,000, in recognition of his superb management of their properties. Many New Yorkers then learned, for the first time, what railroad experts throughout the country had long known, that the transportation of a million people a day in New York's busy streets, without serious friction or public annoyance, is not a matter of chance, but is the result of perhaps the most perfect traffic organization ever created, at the head of which is a man, quiet, forceful, able, with the ability of a great general—a master and at the same time, a friend of men,—himself one for whom in the judgment of his associates almost any higher railroad career is possible.

Thirty years ago Mr. Vreeland, then a lad thirteen years old, was, to use his own humorous, reminiscent phrase, "h'isting ice" on the Hudson River, one of a gang of eighteen or twenty men and boys filling the ice carts for retail city delivery. A picture just brought to light, shows him among the force lined up to be photographed, as a tall, loosely built, hatchet-faced lad in working garb, with a fragment of a smile on his face, as if he could appreciate the contrast of the boy of that day with the man of the future.

How do these things happen? What was the divine spark in this boy's brain and heart that should lift him out of the crowd of the commonplace to the position of responsibility and influence in the world which he now occupies? If my readers could have been present at the interview kindly granted by Mr. Vreeland to the writer, and could have heard him recalling his early life and its many struggles and disappointments with a smile that was often near a tear, they would have gone away feeling that nothing is impossible to him who dares, and, above all else, who *works*, and they would have derived inspiration far greater than can possibly be given in these written words.

"I first entered the railroad business in 1875," said Mr. Vreeland, "shoveling gravel on one of the Long Island Railroad Company's night construction trains. Though this position was humble enough, it was a great thing to me then to feel myself a railroad man, with all that that term implied; and when, after a few months' trial, I was given the job of inspecting ties and roadbed at a dollar a day, I felt that I was well on the road to the presidency.

"One day the superintendent asked my boss if he could give him a reliable man to replace a switchman who had just made a blunder leading to a collision, and had been discharged. The reply was, 'Well, I've got a man named Vreeland here, who will do exactly what you tell him to.' They called me up, and, after a few short, sharp questions from the train-master, I went down to the dreary and desolate marsh near Bushwick, Long Island, and took charge of a switch. For a few days I had to camp out near that switch, in any way that might happen, but finally the officers made up their minds that they could afford me the luxury of a two-by-four flag-house with a stove in it, and I settled down for more railroading.

"The Bushwick station was not far away, and one of the company's division headquarters was there. I soon made the acquaintance of all the officials around that station, and got into their good graces by offering to help them out in their clerical work at any and all times when I was off duty. It was a godsend to them, and exactly what I wanted, for I had determined to get into the inside of the railroad business from bottom to top. Many's the time I have worked till eleven or twelve o'clock at night in that little station, figuring out train receipts and expenses, engine cost and duty, and freight and passenger statistics of all kinds; and, as a result of this work, I quickly acquired a grasp of railroad details in all stages, which few managers possess, for, in one way and another, I got into and through every branch of the business.

"My Bushwick switch was a temporary one, put in for construction purposes only, and, after some months' use, was discontinued, and I was discharged. This did not suit me at all, and I went to one of the officials of the road and told him that I wanted to remain with the Long Island Railroad Company in any capacity whatsoever, and would be obliged to him if he would give me a job. He said, at first, that he hadn't a thing for me to do, but finally added, as if he was ashamed to suggest it, that, if I had a mind to go down on another division and sweep out and dust cars, I might do it. I instantly accepted, and thereby learned the details of another important railroad department.

"Pretty soon they made me brakeman on an early morning train to Hempstead, and then I found that I was worth to the world, after two years of railroad training, just forty dollars a month, *plus* a perquisite or two obtained from running a card-table department in the smoking-cars. I remembered that I paid eighteen dollars of my munificent salary for board and lodging, sent twenty dollars home for the support of my mother and sister, and had two dollars a month and the aforesaid perquisites left for 'luxuries.'

"It was about this time, thus early in my career, that I first came to be known as 'President Vreeland.' An old codger upon the railroad, in talking to me one day, said, in a bantering way: 'Well, I suppose you think your fortune is made, now you have become a brakeman, but let me tell you what will happen. You will be a brakeman about four or five years, and then they will make you a conductor, at about one hundred dollars a month, and there you'll stick all your life, if you don't get discharged.' I responded, rather angrily, 'Do you suppose I am going to be satisfied with remaining a conductor? I mean to be president of a railroad.' 'Ho, ho, ho!' laughed the man. He told the story around, and many a time thereafter the boys slyly placed the word 'President' before my name on official instructions and packages sent to me.

"A conductor on one of the regular trains quarreled one morning with the superintendent and was discharged. I was sent for and told to take out that train. This was jumping me over the heads of many of the older brakemen, and, as a consequence, all the brakemen on that train quit. Others were secured, however, and I ran the train regularly for a good many months.

"Then came an accident one day, for which the engineer and I were jointly responsible. We admitted our responsibility, and were discharged. I went again to the superintendent, however, and, upon a strong plea to be retained in the service, he sent me back to the ranks among the brakemen. I had no complaint to make, but accepted the consequence of my mistake.

"Soon after this, the control of the road passed into other hands. Many were discharged, and I was daily expecting my own 'blue envelope.' One day, I was detailed to act as brakeman on a special which was to convey the president and directors of the road, with invited guests, on a trip over the lines. By that time I had learned the Long Island Railroad in all its branches pretty well; and, in the course of the trip, was called upon to answer a great many questions. The next day I received word that the superintendent wanted to see me. My heart sank within me, for summonses of this kind were ominous in those days, but I duly presented myself at the office and was asked, 'Are you the good-looking brakeman who was on the special yesterday who shows his teeth when he smiles?' I modestly replied that I was certainly on the special yesterday, and I may possibly have partly confirmed the rest of the identification by a smile, for the superintendent, without further questioning, said: 'The president wants to see you, up stairs.'

"I went up, and in due time was shown into the presence of the great man, who eyed me closely for a minute or two, and then asked me abruptly what I was doing. I told him I was braking Number Seventeen. He said: 'Take this letter to your superintendent. It contains a request that he relieve you from duty, and put somebody else in your place. After he has done so, come back here.'

"All this I did, and, on my return to the president, he said, 'Take this letter at once to Admiral Peyron, of the French fleet (then lying in the harbor on a visit of courtesy to this country), and this to General Hancock, on Governor's Island. They contain invitations to each to dine with me to-morrow night at my home in Garden City with their staffs. Get their answers, and, if they say yes, return at once to New York, charter a steamer, call for them to-morrow afternoon, land them at Long Island City, arrange for a special train from Long Island City to Garden City, take them there, and return them after the banquet. I leave everything in your hands. Good day.'

"I suppose this might be considered a rather large job for a common brakeman, but I managed to get through with it without disgracing myself, and apparently to the satisfaction of all concerned. For some time thereafter, I was the president's special emissary on similar matters connected with the general conduct of the business, and while I did not, perhaps, learn so very much about railroading proper, I was put in positions where I learned to take responsibility and came to have confidence in myself.

"The control of the Long Island Railroad again changed hands, and I was again 'let out,' this time for good, so far as that particular road was concerned,—except that, within the last two or three years, I have renewed my acquaintance with it through being commissioned by a banking syndicate in New York City to make an expert examination of its plant and equipment as a preliminary to reorganization.

"This was in 1881, or about that time, and I soon secured a position as conductor on the New York and Northern Railroad, a little line running from One Hundred and Fifty-fifth Street, New York City, to Yonkers. Not to go into tedious detail regarding my experience there, I may say in brief that in course of time

I practically 'ran the road.' After some years, it changed hands (a thing which railways, particularly small ones, often do, and always to the great discomposure of the employees), and the new owners, including William C. Whitney, Daniel S. Lamont, Captain R. Somers Hayes and others, went over the road one day on a special train to visit the property. As I have said, I was then practically running the road, owing to the fact that the man who held the position of general manager was not a railroad man and relied upon me to handle all details, but my actual position was only that of train-master. I accompanied the party, and knowing the road thoroughly, not only physically but also statistically, was able to answer all the questions which they raised. This was the first time I had met Mr. Whitney, and I judge that I made a somewhat favorable impression upon him, for not long after I was created general manager of the road.

"A few months later, I received this telegram:—

'H. H. VREELAND.

'Meet me at Broadway and Seventh Avenue office at two o'clock to-day. WILLIAM C. WHITNEY.'

"I had to take a special engine to do this,

but arrived at two o'clock at the office of the Houston Street, West Street and Pavonia Ferry Railroad Company, which I then knew, in an indistinct sort of way, owned a small horse railway in the heart of New York. After finding that Mr. Whitney was out at lunch, I kicked my heels for a few minutes outside the gate, and then inquired of a man who was seated inside in an exceedingly comfortable chair, when Mr. Whitney and his party were expected, saying, also, that my name was Vreeland, and I had an appointment at two. He replied: 'Oh, are you Mr. Vreeland? Well, here is a letter for you. Mr. Whitney expected to be here at two o'clock, but is a little late.' I took my letter and sat down again outside, thinking that it might possibly contain an appointment for another hour. It was, however, an appointment of quite a different character. It read as follows:—

'Mr. H. H. Vreeland.

'Dear Sir:—At a meeting of the stockholders of the Houston Street, West Street and Pavonia Ferry Railroad Company, held this day, you were unanimously elected a director of the company.

'At a subsequent meeting of the directors, you were unanimously elected president and general manager, your duties to commence immediately.

'Yours truly, C. E. Warren, Secretary.'

"By the time I had recovered from my surprise at learning that I was no longer a steam-railroad, but a street-railroad man, Mr. Whitney and other directors came in, and, after spending about five minutes in introductions, they took up their hats and left, saying, simply, 'Well, Vreeland, you are president; now run the road.' I then set out to learn what kind of a toy railway it was that had come into my charge."

Here Mr. Vreeland's narrative stops, for the rest of the history is well known to the people of New York, and to experts in street railroading throughout the country. The "Whitney syndicate," so called, was then in possession of a few only out of some twenty or more street railway properties in New York City, the Broadway line, however, being one of these, and by far the most valuable. With the immense financial resources of Messrs. Whitney, Widener, Elkins, and their associates, nearly all the other properties were added to the original ones owned by the syndicate, and with the magnificent organizing and executive ability of Mr. Vreeland, there has been built up in New York a street railway system which, while including less than two hundred and fifty miles of track, is actually carrying more than one-half as many passengers each year as are being carried by all the steam railroads of the United States together.

Mr. Vreeland's first work on coming to New York was, naturally, to familiarize himself with the transportation conditions in New York City, and to learn how to handle the peculiarly complex problems involved in street railroading. He first had to gain, also, the confidence of his men, but this is never hard for anyone who is sincerely solicitous for their welfare, and in such sympathy with their work and hardships as a man like himself must have been, with his own past history in mind.

With his hand firmly on the tiller, and with his scheme of organization perfected, he was soon able to take up the larger questions of administration. To Mr. Vreeland is due the credit of initiating and rapidly extending a general free transfer system in New York, by which the public is able to ride from almost any part of the largest city in the country to any other part, for a single five-cent fare, whereas, before the consolidation, two, three, and sometimes four fares would have to be paid for the same ride.

It was upon Mr. Vreeland's recommendation, also, backed by that of F. S. Pearson, the well-known consulting engineer of the Whitney syndicate, that the latter determined to adopt the underground conduit electric system in the reconstruction of the lines. At that time this decision involved the greatest financial and technical courage, since there was but one other road of this kind in existence, and that a small tramway in an Austrian city, while previous American experience with this system had been uniformly unsuccessful.

Not only in street railroading proper, but also in steam railroading, automobile work and the electric lighting field, Mr. Vreeland possesses the absolute confidence of his associates, who rely implicitly upon his judgment, intelligence and business acumen. The recent gift, already referred to, is one only of several which he has received from men who feel that they have made millions through his ability. Although he is not to-day a wealthy man, as men are counted wealthy in New York City, he is certainly well along on the road to millionairedom.

Best of all, however, and what has probably satisfied him most in his life, has been the host

of genuine friendships which he has made, and the strong hold which he has upon the workingman. A strike of the employees of the Metropolitan Street Railway Company is absolutely impossible so long as he remains at the head of the company's affairs, for the men know well that there will be in that position a man who is always fair, and even generous with them, bearing in mind ever his duty to his stockholders; and they know, too, that no injustice will be committed by any of the department heads. Any one of his four or five thousand employees can meet him personally on a question of grievance, and is sure of being treated as a reasonable fellow man. Time and again have labor leaders sought to form an organization of the Metropolitan employees, and as often the men have said in reply, "Not while Vreeland is here,—we know he will treat us fairly."

In a recent address Mr. Vreeland said:—

"No artificial condition can ever, in my judgment, keep down a man who has health, capacity and honesty. You can temporarily interfere with him or make the road to the object of his ambition more difficult, but you cannot stop him. That tyranny is forever dead,

and since its death there has come a great enlightenment to the possessors of power and wealth. Instead of preventing a man from rising, there is not a concern the wide world over that is not to-day eagerly seeking for capable people. The great hunger of the time is for good men, strong men, men capable of assuming responsibility; and there is sharp competition for those who are available."

XXII

How James Whitcomb Riley Came to be Master of the Hoosier Dialect

IT is doubtful if there is in the literary world, to-day, a personage whose boyhood and young manhood can approach in romance and unusual circumstances that of the author of "The Old Swimmin' Hole."

All tradition was against his accomplishing anything in the world. How, indeed, said the good folks of the little town of Greenfield, Indiana, could anything be expected of a boy who cared nothing for school, and deserted it at the first opportunity, to take up a wandering life.

THROWN ON HIS OWN RESOURCES

The boy's father wanted the boy to follow in his footsteps, in the legal profession, and he held out alluring hopes of the possibility of

scaling even greater heights than any to which he had yet attained. Better still,—from the standpoint of the restless James,—he took the youngster with him as he made his circuit from court to court.

These excursions, for they were indeed such to the boy, sowed deep in his heart the seed of a determination to become a nomad; and it was not long until he started out as a strolling sign-painter, determined upon the realization of his ideals.

Oftentimes business was worse than dull, and, on one occasion, hunger drove him for recourse to his wits, and lo, he blossomed forth as a "blind sign-painter," led from place to place by a little boy, and showered with sympathy and trade in such abundance that he could hardly bear the thought of the relinquishment of a pretense so ingenious and successful, entered on at first as a joke.

Then came another epoch. The young man fell in with a patent-medicine man, with whom he joined fortunes, and here the young Indianian, who had been scribbling more or less poetry, found a new use for his talent; for his duties in the partnership were to beguile the people with joke and song, while his co-worker

plied the sales of his cure-all. There were many times when, but for his fancy, the young poet might have seen his audience dwindle rapidly away. It was while thus engaged, that he had the opportunities which enabled him to master thoroughly the Hoosier dialect.

When the glamor of the patent-medicine career had faded somewhat, the nomadic Riley joined a band of strolling Thespians, and, in this brief portion of his life, after the wont of players of his class, played many parts.

At length, he began to give a little more attention to his literary work; and, later, obtained a place on an Indianapolis paper, where he published his first poems, and they won their author almost instant success.

WHY HE LONGED TO BE A BAKER

When I drew Mr. Riley out to talk still further of those interesting days, and the strange experiences which came to him therein, the conversation finally turned on the subject of his youthful ambition.

"I think my earliest remembered one," he said, "was an insatiate longing to become a baker. I don't know what prompted it, unless it were the visions of the mountains of alluring 'goodies,' which, as they are ranged in the windows of the pastry shops, appear doubly tempting to the youth whose mother not only counsels moderation, but enforces it.

"Next, I imagined that I would like to become a showman of some sort.

"Then, my shifting fancy conjured up visions of how grand it would be to work as a painter, and decorate houses and fences in glowing colors.

"Finally, as I grew a little older, there returned my old longing to become an actor. When, however, my dreams were realized, and I became a member of a traveling theatrical company, I found that the life was full of hardships, with very little chance of rising in the world.

"I never had any literary ambition whatever, so far as I can remember. I wrote, primarily, simply because I desired to have something to read, and could not find selections that exactly suited me. Gradually I found a demand for my little efforts springing up; and so my brother, who could write legibly transcribed them."

James Whitcomb Riley

PERSISTENCE

At this point I asked Mr. Riley his idea of the prime requisites for success in the field of letters.

"The most essential factor," he replied "is persistence,—the determination never to allow your energy or enthusiasm to be dampened by the discouragement that must inevitably come. I believe that he is richer for the battle with the world, in any vocation, who has great determination and little talent, rather than his seemingly more fortunate brother with great talent, perhaps, but little determination. As for the field of literature, I cannot but express my conviction that meteoric flights, such as have been taken, of recent years, by some young writers with whose names almost everybody is familiar, cannot fail to be detrimental, unless the man to whom success comes thus early and suddenly is an exceptionally evenly-balanced and sensible person.

"Many persons have spoken to me about Kipling's work, and remarked how wonderful a thing is the fact that such achievements could have been possible for a man comparatively so young. I say, not at all. What do we find when we investigate? Simply that Kipling began working on a newspaper when he was only thirteen years of age, and he has been toiling ever since. So you see, even that case confirms my theory that every man must be 'tried in the fire,' as it were.

"He may begin early or late—and in some cases the fight is longer than in others—but of one thing I feel sure, that there is no short-cut to permanent, self-satisfying success in literature, or anything else."

TWENTY YEARS OF REJECTED MANUSCRIPTS

"Mr. Riley," I asked, "would you mind saying something about the obstacles over which you climbed to success?"

"I am afraid it would not be a very pleasant story," he replied. "A friend came to me once, completely heartbroken, saying that his manuscripts were constantly returned, and that he was the most miserable wretch alive. I asked him how long he had been trying? 'Three years,' he said. 'My dear man,' I answered, laughing, 'go on, keep on trying till you have spent as many years at it as I did.' 'As many as you did!' he exclaimed. 'Yes, as long as I did.' 'What, you struggled for years!' 'Yes, sir; through years, through sleepless nights, through almost hopeless days. For twenty years I tried to get into one magazine; back came my manuscripts eternally. I kept on. In the twentieth year, that magazine accepted one of my articles.'

"I was not a believer in the theory that one man does a thing much easier than any other man. Continuous, unflagging effort, persistence and determination will win. Let not the man be discouraged who has these."

"What would you advise one to do with his constantly rejected manuscript?" I asked.

"Put it away awhile; then remodel it. Young writers make the mistake I made."

"What mistake?" I asked.

"Hurrying a manuscript off before it was dry from my pen, as if the world were just waiting for that article and must have it. Now it can hardly be drawn from me with a pair of tweezers. Yes, lay it aside awhile. Reread. There is a rotten spot somewhere. Perhaps it is full of hackneyed phrases, or lacks in sparkle and originality. Search, examine, rewrite, simplify. Make it lucid. *I am glad, now, that my manuscripts did come back.* Presently I would discover this defect, then that.

Perhaps three or four sleepless nights would show my failure to be in an unsymmetrical arrangement of the verses.

"See these books?" he said, rapping upon the book case with the back of his hand. "Classics! but of what do they tell? Of the things of their own day. Let us write the things of our day. Literary fields exhausted! Nonsense. If we write well enough, ours will be the classics of to-morrow. Our young Americans have, right at hand, the richest material any country ever offered. Let them be brave and work in earnest."

A COLLEGE EDUCATION

Answering other questions, the poet said:— "A college education for the aspirant for literary success is, of course, an advantage, provided he does not let education foster a false culture that will lead him away from the ideals he ought to cling to.

"There is another thing that the young man in any artistic pursuit must have a care for; and that is, to be practical. This is a practical world, and it is always ready to take advantage of this sort of people: so that one must try to cultivate a practical business sense as well as an artistic sense. We have only a few men like Rudyard Kipling and F. Hopkinson Smith, who seem to combine these diverse elements of character in just the right proportions; but I believe that it is unfortunate for the happiness and peace of mind of our authors, and artists, and musicians, that we have not more of them."

RILEY'S POPULARITY

Riley's poetry is popular because it goes right to the feelings of the people. He could not have written as he does, but for the schooling of that wandering life, which gave him an insight into the struggle for existence among the great unnumbered multitude of his fellow men. He learned in his travels and journeys, in his hard experience as a strolling sign-painter and patent-medicine peddler the freemasonry of poverty. His poems are natural; they are those of a man who feels as he writes. As Thoreau painted nature in the woods, and streams, and lakes, so Riley depicts the incidents of everyday life, and brightens each familiar lineament with that touch that makes all the world akin.